The Return of the River

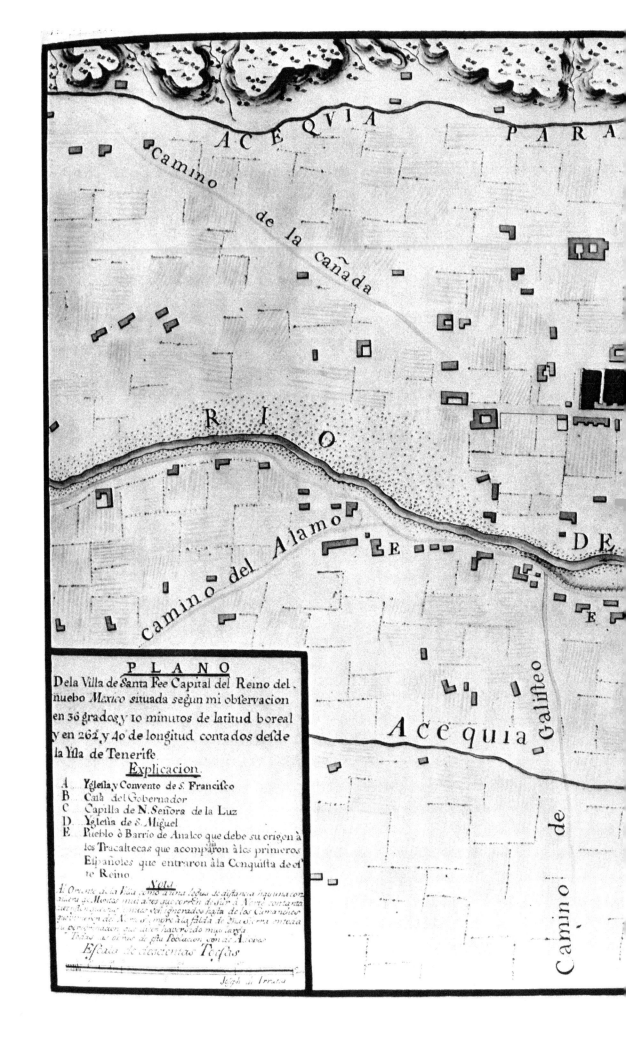

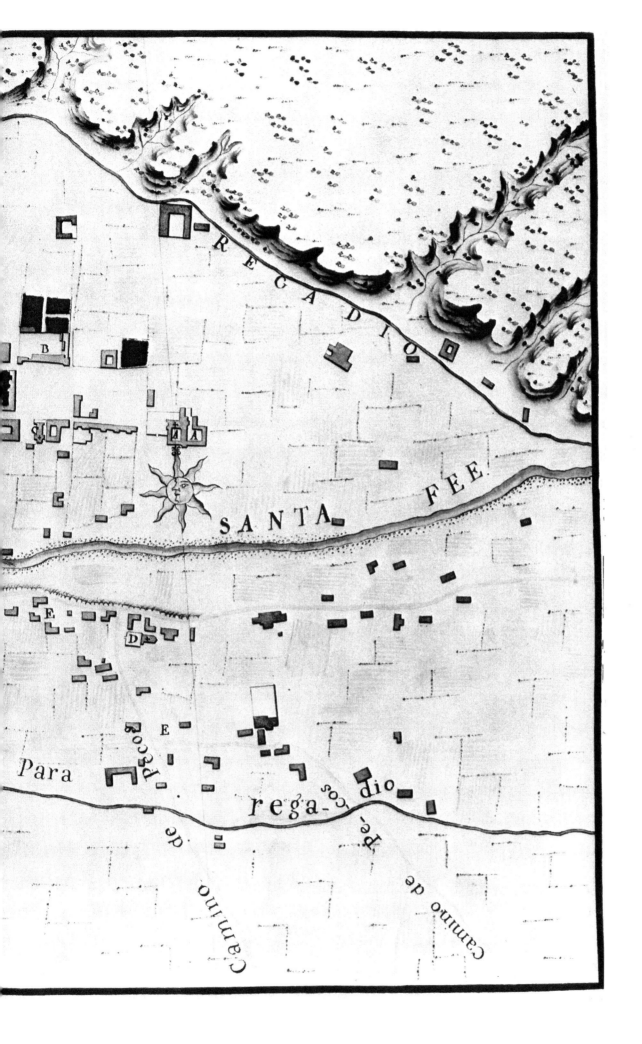

The Return of the River

Writers, Scholars, and Citizens
Speak on Behalf of the Santa Fe River

Edited by
A. Kyce Bello

SANTA FE

Sunstone books may be purchased for educational, business, or sales promotional use.
For information please write: Special Markets Department, Sunstone Press,
P.O. Box 2321, Santa Fe, New Mexico 87504-2321.

Book and Cover design ~Vicki Ahl
Body typeface ~ Book Antiqua and Freestyle script
Printed on acid free paper

Library of Congress Cataloging-in-Publication Data

The return of the river : writers, scholars, and citizens speak on behalf of the Santa Fe
River / edited by A. Kyce Bello.
     p. cm.
  ISBN 978-0-86534-781-6 (softcover : alk. paper)
  1. Santa Fe River (N.M.)--Literary collections. 2. Environmental protection--New
Mexico--Santa Fe--Literary collections. 3. American literature--New Mexico--Santa
Fe. I. Bello, A. Kyce, 1981-
  PS571.N6R47 2011
  810.8'036--dc22

                          2010051184

WWW.SUNSTONEPRESS.COM
SUNSTONE PRESS / POST OFFICE BOX 2321 / SANTA FE, NM 87504-2321 /USA
(505) 988-4418 / ORDERS ONLY (800) 243-5644 / FAX (505) 988-1025

The Return of the River

Contents

I
History and Memory ~ 85

II
Sustenance and Loss ~ 85

///
Resurgence ~141

Acknowledgements

*T*he *Return of the River* was inspired in part by the anthology *Testimony: Writers of the West Speak on Behalf of Utah Wilderness,* compiled by Stephen Trimble and Terry Tempest Williams. *Testimony* was the first in a handful of recent collections that use literature to defend the natural world. These books — eloquent, persuasive, and effective agents of change — demonstrate that art and activism need not be exclusive of each other. It has been my extraordinary privilege to follow in that vein and bring together a community of voices from Santa Fe to mobilize support for the river that nourishes us daily.

My heartfelt gratitude goes to each of the fine writers, ecologists, historians, activists, and poets who enthusiastically contributed work to this book. You gave out of gratitude to the waters that sustain your creative life, and I pray that those waters nurture your work so that it bears many, many sweet fruits. It goes without saying but nevertheless must be said: without you, this book would never have been. Thank you.

Special thanks to: Suzanne Otter for the beautiful cover art; Tara Plewa for help with images and figures; Miriam Sagan for advice; The Mirus Foundation for support and guidance; Rahmaneh and Tomas Meyers for illuminating the myriad ways in which water sustains us; Benjamin Allison for counsel; the wonderful archivists and librarians who assisted with research and granted permission to reprint material; Robert Findling of the Nature Conservancy; the team at Sunstone Press who gave this book its form; and the many others who helped bring this book into being "one way or another."

Thanks also to the Santa Fe River Commission for their generous support, and to all commissioners past and present that have worked to bring the river back to life. My appreciation goes out to all who have contributed to, or served on, river committees, task forces, and associations over the last few decades, as well as the many citizens who never stopped believing in the river's importance in our lives. This book is only the most recent effort in a long history of activism on behalf of the river, and I gratefully acknowledge all that has been done by these many dedicated individuals. May their efforts be soon rewarded.

Foreword

David Coss
Mayor of Santa Fe

*I*t is my distinct pleasure to add a few words to this collection of voices speaking on behalf of the Santa Fe River. I am excited to be Mayor of Santa Fe at a time when residents are not only conscious, but fully accepting of the challenge of leaving a sustainable community to future generations of our 400-year-old city.

As a boy growing up in Santa Fe, the river — a resource that had provided joy and sustenance for centuries — was mostly ignored or treated as a problem by post-WWII engineering and development practices. I didn't know it then, but our river was rapidly dying. To meet the community's needs for water, we dammed the river and drilled wells in the alluvial aquifers along the river with no thought about conservation. While depleting the flow and the aquifer, we channeled our river so that development could crowd ever closer to its banks. We paved giant parking lots for new malls and directed pollution toward the river. As the water table dropped, the Santa Fe River eroded over 25 feet and nearly disappeared from view.

How ironic that the environmental consciousness that we were developing as a community and nation in the 1960s and 1970s led to the protection of rivers and streams around the State of New Mexico by the federal Clean Water Act while providing no protection for our river in Santa Fe. By the 1990s, the Santa Fe River was considered a storm water chute, not a river.

Fortunately, the river was not forgotten by all. Through the 1980s and 1990s small groups of residents worked and lobbied to restore it. Though a living river was often dismissed as a pipe dream, activists who believed in the cultural, ecological and historical importance of the Santa Fe River kept working. A master plan was developed, the Santa Fe Watershed Association was formed, and federal, state and local governments came together to study and improve the river and surrounding watershed.

Today, due to many decades of work and perseverance, we have a living river above Santa Fe in the National Forest and below Santa Fe in the La Cienega area. The challenge before us is the revival of a living river in the urban area throughout the City of Santa Fe. A growing number of residents, businesses and community organizations are coming together and have shown unprecedented action in making the dream of a living river a reality.

The Santa Fe Watershed Association has partnered with local businesses to clean and maintain sections of the river. The City of Santa Fe hired a River and Watershed Coordinator and reinstated the River Commission. We have contracted with ¡YouthWorks! on erosion control projects, helping young people not only respect and protect the environment in which they live, but also to develop job skills that will help them succeed in the future. A new segment of the River Trail was recently completed, and this summer we will begin river channel restoration and trail construction from the Camino Alire Bridge to Frenchy's Park. Santa Fe County, working with citizen groups began restoration of the river channel in Agua Fria below the Santa Isidro Crossing.

Meanwhile, hundreds of people participate in river clean-ups and festivals. Santa Feans have become the most efficient water users in the United States, and rightly call for some of their conservation efforts to benefit the Santa Fe River. We have taken the step of becoming the first City in the state to set aside water for flow and the creation of a living river in town; in 2009, we released 700 acre feet into the river and plan to keep a minimum flow through the summer months.

Today, thanks to the people of Santa Fe, the river is no longer dying. It is returning as a valued community resource which will connect our community and serve as an indicator not only of the state of our watershed but also the health of our entire city. Children, youth, parents and seniors can all look to the river now and see their community becoming more alive, more resilient and more beautiful. Thank you to all the people who have kept the river alive and who will continue to work to make the Santa Fe River a living part of the community once again.

Flash flood on the Santa Fe River, 1957. Photograph by Richard Kulisheck.

Preface: Re-storying the River

> To restore any place, we must also begin to re-story it, to make it the lesson of our legends, festivals, and seasonal rites. By replenishing the land with our stories, we let the wild voices around us guide the restoration work we do. Stories will outlast us.
> —Gary Paul Nabhan

In the spring of 2007, the Santa Fe River reached an all time low. As snowmelt briefly flooded its dry bed, luring animals to its banks and recharging thirsty plants, the organization American Rivers declared the Santa Fe River the most endangered river in the country. Two months later, as the supply of snowmelt ran out and the riverbed dried up once again, the New Mexico Historic Preservation Alliance named our river one of the twelve most endangered sites in the state. Dry for decades, eroded, barren, trashed, and all but forgotten, one might say the Santa Fe River was lucky to be merely endangered and not hopelessly extinct.

While unfortunate, these designations remain a call to action for Santa Feans to act on behalf of our neglected river. The Santa Fe River's condition is the responsibility of not only the politicians and developers, but of we ordinary people who have become habituated to its emptiness. We are accustomed to forgetting, and often don't even know what we've lost, let alone how to repair it. Of all the political, economic, and legal hurdles facing the river's restoration, the task of collectively remembering that the river's fate is our own is perhaps the greatest challenge before us. It is a challenge that the written word seems uniquely suited to address.

The premise of *The Return of the River* is that by re-storying the Santa Fe River—by bringing it back to life in our hearts and minds—we can begin to work towards its physical restoration. Ultimately, our ability to imagine a living river is a critical step in manifesting one. This is why our stories, poetry, songs, and art are a necessary part of breathing life back into the Santa Fe River. I believe this kind of praise and honoring feed it in a vital way. For a river can flow with water and still be invisible and neglected if it doesn't live inside us. Just as the land we inhabit shapes our narratives about who we are, our stories inevitably shape the land.

The Return of the River offers an alternative narrative to the dominant story of the river's ruin, and celebrates the river as the ecological, social, and historic heart of Santa Fe. The contributors to this book speak in diverse ways about why a living river matters. Their words range from scholarly to deeply personal, practical to whimsical. By moving us from ignorance and despair towards awareness and hope, these writers help us take the first step in reviving our river.

While this book was first inspired by the Santa Fe River's endangered status, it has been sustained by the river's potential to recover and live again. It is possible to heal our river by releasing sufficient water to it and to prevent further erosion by reshaping the crumbling riverbanks. As individuals, we can take steps that translate into change. We can conserve water—and then call our city councilors to demand the unused water be released to the river. We can donate to the city's River Fund and become members of the Santa Fe Watershed Association. We can join our neighbors in picking up trash and planting trees along the riverbank. We can walk in or along the river, reacquainting ourselves with the land we call home.

Most of all, we can tell our stories about the river, whether they are tales of how it has quenched our thirst or left us yearning for more. Each of us has the power to change the story we tell about the river from one of loss and resignation to one of beauty and abundance. Let us begin to tell the story of how we brought the river back to life.

—A. Kyce Bello
Santa Fe, 2010

America's Most Endangered Rivers The Santa Fe River

2007 Report by American Rivers

For over 20 years, the national advocacy group American Rivers has released an annual report on the ten most endangered rivers in the country. The report spotlights rivers facing not only serious threats but also the potential for renewal. In 2007, the Santa Fe River topped the list, drawing national attention to our dry riverbed and fueling local momentum for a living river. By illustrating the consequences of letting our river run dry, and offering clear arguments in favor of allocating water for environmental flow, the report is an excellent introduction to the issues around our endangered river and its restoration.

To an entire generation of Santa Fe residents, the city's namesake river is not a river at all for most of the year, but a dry, weed-choked ditch. Dams for the city's water supply lock the river before it can leave the mountains which give it birth, while wells throughout the city have lowered the water table to the point where it no longer sustains the river. The city, county and state governments are investing millions of dollars for parks and trails along the river channel in the name of "river restoration" — but stream restoration without water is no restoration at all. There is an unparalleled opportunity to bring the river back to life as the city government considers the option of a flowing river. The city of Santa Fe, which controls most of the river's water, needs to restore at least some flow to the river, even as it develops a water budget and permanent commitment to restoration that sustain the community and recapture the many benefits of a healthy river.

The River

The Santa Fe River begins in the Sangre de Cristo Mountains and flows 42 miles before reaching the Rio Grande, but this relatively small river is steeped in history. The Spanish established their administrative capital beside the river in 1610, amid several pueblo villages. During the Spanish colonial period and into the mid-20th century the river served a complex network of irrigation canals (called acequias) supporting more than 1,000 acres of irrigated cropland.

The Santa Fe River was featured on the cover of America's Most Endangered Rivers 2007 report. © Julie West/American Rivers. Used with permission.

Long-time residents remember fishing for trout in the river in downtown Santa Fe, building swimming holes and even ice-skating. But ask them precisely when the fishing stopped and the river dried up, and most can't recall. Over time, the river was turned off and on according to the demands of the city's water system and gradually the river was "off" more than it was "on." Fishing and swimming disappeared, and the community grew accustomed to a dry river channel.

For the past 20 years, the river has been used to fill the reservoirs in the upper reaches and as a drainage ditch to evacuate stormwater in the lower reaches. In addition, extensive urban growth in the Santa Fe area has rapidly increased demand for existing water supplies. In many reaches, the Santa Fe has ceased to function as a river, and the riparian ecosystem has largely dried up.

The results of the city's long neglect of its namesake river can be seen in the dry ditch littered with trash, overgrown with weeds and deeply eroded. Native vegetation along the river is in trouble and invasive species like Siberian elm are pushing out native cottonwoods and willows.

Looking at the dry riverbed today, it is hard to imagine that lush meadows and fine land for wildlife, crops and livestock once lined the course of the Santa Fe. Interlaced with old main stem acequias and secondary ditches called sangrías, the deep-rooted community supported by this system of veins and capillaries was a living embodiment of the Spanish saying, "*El agua es la sangre de la tierra*" — "the water is the lifeblood of the land."

Pueblo ruins beside the river document its life-giving power stretching deep into the past, long before the arrival of Spanish conquistadores. Among current residents, many can trace their lineage back to those same soldiers, officers in the army of Spain who were awarded land along the river for their service. It was a claim that would last for generations.

Lining the banks of the flowing river was a vibrant bosque, a forest of cottonwoods and willows, a resource for both wildlife and people alike. Beyond the bosque, meadows supported decades of sustainable grazing and the river watered orchards, alfalfa fields and corn. This crop, both food and a powerful symbol to native peoples in the region, is still an integral part of the culture of the pueblos and acequias of northern New Mexico.

In the town of Agua Fria—Spanish for "cool water"—the river below Santa Fe gave life to a small community that traces its roots back to the early 17th century. Then the lifeblood of this land disappeared, and with it much of the community and culture it had watered. The town of Agua Fria is a shadow of its former self, parched along with the riverbed. Without a flowing river, the water table sank, and wells had to reach deeper and deeper to find moisture. Without water in the river, sand and gravel miners chewed at the riverbed, and periodic flash floods ravaged the riverbanks that had lost their protective mantle of vegetation.

This rich life that the Santa Fe River once sustained is hardly ancient history; people alive today in Agua Fria remember the running river and the vibrant community it supported.

Nor is it an impossible dream. Whenever there is a bounteous period of rain or snow, and the reservoir gates are opened upstream, the river responds. This spring, following a favorable winter snowpack, the river may be flowing again, reminding New Mexicans what a living Santa Fe River once was, and could be again.

The Threat

The river has not had a fully natural flow of water since 1881, when the first dam was built to secure a steadier water supply for a growing Santa Fe. A series of successively larger dams came and went over the years, and today the river is fully impounded by twin reservoirs. The city of Santa Fe owns the dams, and holds the use rights to most of the surface water. The few remaining acequias also hold a small portion of the surface water rights. Both city-owned and private groundwater wells along the river extract water from the aquifer. No instream flow rights exist to support uses like recreation, or to protect important native fish and wildlife populations.

The major threat to the future of the Santa Fe River is the outdated assumption that a flowing river is a waste of water. Unfortunately, this attitude has kept the city from developing and implementing water efficiency steps and other measures that could guarantee enough water both for tap water and for the many other things the people of Santa Fe once enjoyed about the river.

The modern science of river management emphasizes natural river dynamics and water cycles. Removing water from the river channel destroys not only water-dependent plants and animals, but also diminishes subsurface aquifers and local springs, some of which have disappeared entirely. All of these suffer when Santa Fe treats its river as an extension of the city's plumbing system that can be turned on and off (at the reservoirs) and as a dumping ground for polluted runoff in the lower reaches. And while Santa Fe has shown real leadership in the Southwest on water conservation, the city has not implemented a number of important steps that would mean more water for the river. For example, Santa Fe needs significantly better stormwater management, more efficient landscape irrigation and systems to capture more of the rain that falls on city roofs, parking lots and roads.

What's at Stake

Without water in the river, the people of Santa Fe cannot reap the myriad economic, environmental, aesthetic, social and spiritual benefits a living river provides. The city now has a chance to restore the river to the forefront of community life. Restoring flows to the river would provide not only a healthy ecosystem, but also a place for residents of Santa Fe to rejuvenate, visitors to enjoy and children to play. Tourism and art, which have attracted worldwide attention and serve as the two central pillars of the local economy, would benefit from a healthy Santa Fe River.

Local governments and non-profit groups are already working on a river trail system along the historic Camino Real, which ran along the Santa Fe River from the Rio Grande to the Spanish colonial capital in Santa Fe. A proposal for Santa Fe's historic downtown features the river as the centerpiece of a new park and community space. A natural, flowing Santa Fe River is an essential aspect of these public spaces. Fortunately, a number of coinciding factors—from Mayor David Coss' promise of a "living river" to Governor Bill Richardson's declaration of 2007 as the "Year of Water" in New Mexico—have set the stage for the river's revival.

What Must Be Done

During the coming months, the community of Santa Fe has an unprecedented opportunity to bring back a living, flowing Santa Fe River. The city already has taken positive steps to lay out a long-range plan for flow restoration: First, the city council will decide whether to include a provision for a small flow in the river as part of its new long-range water plan. Second, the city plans to initiate the Santa Fe River Fund, a private-public match program to purchase water rights for the river, which, over the next decade or so, would guarantee permanent water allocation for the river, legal water rights for instream flows.

Both of these steps are already in the works and together set the stage for eventually restoring the Santa Fe River. But planning for the long term, while necessary, is not sufficient. Indeed, Santa Fe has seen past goals for flow restoration derailed by the relentless water demands of new development. Long term planning won't bring back the Santa Fe River unless those plans include near-term commitments to instream flow, linked with clear, measurable goals for how much water the city will commit to a living river. In the coming year, the city needs to take two crucial, short-term steps to bring the river back to life:

- First, and most urgently, the city must explicitly allocate some minimal releases to the river as immediate relief for the river ecosystem. Putting water in the river now is an essential down payment on the city's long-term plans.

- Second, the city must make good on that down payment by setting and implementing a permanent water allocation for the river, incorporating both science and community desires to arrive at a significant and sustainable flow recommendation. The city may choose to scale up gradually to this recommended water allocation level, but it is essential to set a quantifiable target now, even if it would be realized only later, as part of the long-range water plan.

The future of the Santa Fe River is largely in the hands of the city of Santa Fe, which holds the water rights and controls dam releases. The city needs to make a clear commitment to restoring flow to the river, and then take advantage of a healthy Santa Fe River in planning and envisioning the future of the community.

1

History and Memory

The song of the river ends
not at her banks,
but in the hearts of those
who have loved her.

— Buffalo Joe

Blue Winding, Blue Way

Valerie Martínez

I tell you—City, City, City—a story you told me—brown eyes, green eyes, black—in the days of snow drifts, mini-skirts, nothing beyond Richard's Ave. The center of earth was a patch of land with our house, the backyard, arroyo humming over the reddish concrete wall, and one immortal turtle. The neighbor's immense ham radio antenna and Mr. Chang hunched to static and metal under the morning buzz of Osage Ave. We went to school in pick-ups and dented sedans, or workmen showed up to build vigas in the big room that swelled our home, Alfonso saying, Linda, get me that bucket and ¿donde está tu mama? Me saying, at the grocery store buying tubs of ice cream, you know, those big ones? Get me, ice cream, you know took to the air over the rooftops to Frenchy's Field. We weren't supposed to go there—he'll shoot, you know—and I imagined the old man hunched somewhere near the water, listening. In those days the Santa Fe River ran and sang. It's true? you ask, staring at the empty bed, dust rising at the dead end of Avenida Cristobal Colón. There was water? Now, we dream of blue winding, blue way along West Alameda—barbershop, co-op, health clinic. The clog and cough of St. Francis Drive. Back then there were cars and wanderers and children just like now—towheads, dark braids, dirty cuffs—rolled up with all of us on the days of markets and parades along San Francisco and Palace Ave. Hmmm went the setting sun and you really could get fry bread for a quarter after walking down Washington Street from Fort Marcy after Zozobra burned. Now I drive downtown where the acequia crosses Closson and Maynard, stutters along Water St. and sings the parallels of East Alameda and Canyon Road. Like a whisper, it lays itself down between Camino del Monte Sol and Camino Cabra, two streets with the river in-between—one with her skirt trailing southwest to the Paseo Real, the other reaching her fingernail moons to the foothills. And the river itself, dream of p'oe tsawa, flushed from the red burn of the Sangres, running headlong downhill into this city of ours, then and now, with her canciónes encantadas—with her blue, with her brown mouth open.

⌒

Valerie Martínez is a poet, translator, teacher, playwright/librettist, and collaborative artist. Her books include *World to World*, *A Flock of Scarlet Doves*, and *Each and Her*. She is Executive Director of *Littleglobe, Inc.*, an artist-run non-profit that collaborates with communities on art and community dialogue projects. Valerie served as Poet Laureate for the City of Santa Fe, New Mexico from 2008 - 2010.

Celebrating
the Santa Fe River Watershed

Jack Loeffler

Santa Fe Canyon pierces the foothills of the Sangre de Cristos, the eastern arm of the Southern Rockies that together with their western arm, the San Juan, Tusas, and Jemez Mountains, embrace the northern reaches of the Rio Grande. Santa Fe Canyon cradles the streambed of the Santa Fe River, a frequently abandoned meander that occasionally flows into the Rio Grande, which itself marks the course of the second largest rift of its kind in the world. To paraphrase the late, great Aldo Leopold, thinking like a watershed is possibly the clearest way to understand homeland.

It is thought by some scholars that four hundred years ago, *La Villa Real de la Santa Fé de San Francisco de Asís*, was laid out geo-mythically by Tlascalan Indians who had accompanied Juan de Oñate northward from Zacatecas. These Mexican Indians had an understanding of the appropriate way to physically craft a community within the context of surrounding habitat. Mountains lie to the east, water is present in relative abundance, the westerly sun showers its light, life is nurtured, the landscape is spiritually revered, the spirit of place is honored. Thus Santa Fe was born and has lingered long and in beauty.

Indeed the Santa Fe River has been the aquatic lifeline of not just the human community, but also the surrounding biotic community within the geophysical cradle that provides the structural cohesion of this watershed. The myriad life forms, most of which are not visible to the naked eye, collectively generate an élan that is felt throughout the watershed by all living creatures whose sensitivities are honed in favor of survival.

The great Russian geographer/philosopher Pyotr Kropotkin contended that evolution of species owes far more to mutual cooperation than mutual antagonism. He favored political decentralization as the most just and intelligent way for the human species to comport itself. Subsequent to Kropotkin, the bioregional movement stirred within our species as a means of comporting ourselves favorably within our respective ecosystems. It may be difficult for an individual human to envision the home bioregion, but one can readily identify the home watershed with only modest effort. The Santa Fe River watershed is tiny relative to the Rio Grande watershed of which it is part, yet it is vitally important both to itself and to the greater biogeographic continuum. Biogeography, the study of plant and animal communities over space and time, is a most splendid field of science. It has been known to lead the practitioner into a state of consciousness that is utterly appropriate for our time on the planet.

We are presently dominated by an erroneous economic paradigm that favors money far beyond intrinsic worth. We see turning habitat into money as the fundament of fiscal wisdom. We have long since secularized habitat, landscape, and waterways in a way that is a horrendous affront to the sensibilities of our Puebloan neighbors who have successfully survived in small autonomous communities wherein the seasonal cycles are celebrated in great ceremonials that honor the spirit of place. They have much to teach us about attitude.

If we can come to regard ourselves as members of the biotic community privileged to inhabit the Santa Fe River watershed, to perceive it as homeland wherein we become utterly familiar with its biotic and geophysical characteristics, to understand intuitively the elements of its own story, to become truly conscious of the ramifications of our human presence and act accordingly on behalf of the greatest good, our homeland may yet survive the juggernaut of factors that threaten so much of our planetary ecosystem. In my opinion, we must nurture a collective spiritual connection to homeland. To again cite Aldo Leopold, "Obligations have no meaning without conscience, and the problem we face is the extension of the social conscience from people to land."

~~~

Jack Loeffler moved to northern New Mexico in 1962 and has spent time as a sandal-maker, fire-lookout, environmentalist, curator, aural historian, sound collage artist, radio producer, and writer. His most recent book is entitled *Healing the West: Voices of Culture and Habitat*. He is currently producing a new radio series and book, both entitled *Thinking Like a Watershed*. In 2009, Loeffler was a recipient of the New Mexico Governor's Award for Excellence in the Arts.

Introduction to the Archaeology of the Santa Fe River Valley

Cherie Scheick and Frances Levine

When Spanish settlers arrived in New Mexico in the late sixteenth century and established their first capitol at the Tewa pueblo of Ohkay Owingeh near the confluence of the Rio Grande and the Rio Chama, Santa Fe was used but no longer occupied by Pueblo people. Tewa and Keres Pueblo people nonetheless remember this place. Today, Tewa oral history tells them they lived on both sides of the Santa Fe River where the Spanish *villa* soon grew up, eventually overtaking their earlier fields and homes. Just as in the fourteenth and fifteenth centuries, Pueblo occupations similarly overshadowed earlier inhabitants, whose villages and activity areas dot the high terraces above the river and line the many Santa Fe River tributaries.

The Santa Fe area is part of what archaeologists call the Tano province, a cultural area located entirely within the Santa Fe River and Galisteo Creek basin of the Rio Grande drainage in north-central New Mexico. Before European contact and in the early historic periods, the Tano people, that is, ancestral southern Tewa Pueblo people, occupied all but the southwest corner of this province. By A.D. 900 the Tano province was a developing center of Pueblo culture, and between A.D. 1300 and 1680 it became a major population center. The Santa Fe River valley dominates the north half of this province.

Although long known and understood by the area's historic Tewa inhabitants, the Santa Fe area's older history has become more apparent in recent years. As Santa Fe expands and experiences a modern building boom, archaeologists continually uncover evidence of an older center under our historic city. Every shovel turned in the ground around Santa Fe uncovers artifacts that are evidence of this older history—the history of the ancestral Pueblo people who were here before the Spanish—and still deeper remains that date back to the earliest hunters and gatherers.

The history of these original inhabitants is largely unrecorded and differs perhaps from how we traditionally define history. Nonetheless, parts of this history are told through archaeological research that complements the remembered stories and prayers of the ancient people's descendants now living in the Tewa pueblos north and the Keres pueblos south of the city.

The Rito Santa Fe. Photograph by A. Kyce Bello.

Understanding Settlement in the Santa Fe River Valley

The Santa Fe River valley and its surrounding environs contain a wide variety of archaeological sites that encompass nearly 12,000 years of use. That use fluctuated between long- and short-term stays, but the Santa Fe area was never abandoned. Archaeologists once considered the pre-thirteenth-century Santa Fe River valley, like the northern middle Rio Grande valley in general, largely peripheral to the major developments of such centers as Chaco Canyon, Mimbres, Mesa Verde, and the Hopi and Zuni areas. This belief grew out of 100 years of investigations that focused on tracing the origins of particular traits, such as architectural and ceramic variation and the Katchina cult, back to a presumed Pueblo "heartland." In part, this was a direct consequence of the limited studies conducted at a few very large sites of hundreds, if not thousands, of rooms. Archaeologists presumed that these sites showed occupational continuity with the historic pueblos. Combined, the preoccupation with the historic pueblos and the absence of systematic archaeological work in the area perpetuated the myth of northern New Mexico's marginality.

For the Santa Fe River valley, the increased archaeological work over the last 20 years has brought a fuller, richer understanding of the complexity of the area's archaeological sites and the people whose past they represent. Because of that work, we know populations were living in and using the area well before the big pueblos of the A.D. 1200s. We know these earlier groups lived more lightly on the land, thus leaving less visible reminders. We know the coming together of populations into the large villages actually began before the thirteenth-century.

Over time, area populations grew in concert with changing environments and social circumstances, leading to the "population explosion" evidenced in the archaeological record by increases in both the number and sizes of habitation settlements circa A.D. 1200. Although widely debated, most archaeologists agree the area's population explosion came from a combination of in situ growth and some immigration from the west and northwest. The region's population continued to increase up to the late A.D.1200s and early 1300s, after which major settlements occurred in the Santa Fe area. Area populations continued to grow up until A.D. 1350, when the area's people began consolidating into fewer and even larger pueblos at lower elevations in well-watered areas.

All these changes combined eventually placed subsistence and cultural stresses on area populations, whose responses were both cultural and economic. Communities became even larger and new ways of holding the communities together emerged, such as formalized religion and sophisticated ceremonialism. Just as importantly, subsistence and settlement strategies intensified and established trade networks shifted directions. These events and the associated changes in group and population composition eventually led to the formation of the large Protohistoric Pueblo communities in the middle to late fifteenth centuries. This was also the approximate distribution of the Pueblo communities at the time of first contact with the Spanish exploratory expeditions of the middle sixteenth century.

Archaeological Patterns Over Time

To document, describe, explain, and place in time patterns observed in Santa Fe River valley archaeology, archaeologists group visual evidence into broad cultural-temporal periods to talk about shifts in the use of land and water and in the forms of communities through time. We distinguish the successive periods by changes in artifacts, architecture, settlement patterns, and land use. For the northern Rio Grande, the pre-contact sequence begins with the Paleoindian period and ends with the Classic period.

Paleoindian (10,000/9500 B.C. – 5500/6000 B.C.) sites, typically characterized by the presence of large diagnostic projectile point forms and specialized scrapers found either in isolation or in association with small scatters of chipped stone artifacts, represent the earliest remains of human occupation in the American Southwest. Paleoindian groups were highly mobile, moving across large regions and leaving little material remains behind. Campsites occur in grassy basins or plains around now-dried lakes, while home sites or base camps are in areas near fresh water. Archaeological evidence suggests climatic change primarily was responsible for differences in technology, settlement organization and diet through time during the Paleo-Indian period.

The **Archaic period** (5500/6000 B.C. – A.D. 500/600) is both a time period and a way of life characterized by broad-spectrum foraging of plant seed resources and hunting of both small and large game. We attribute this shift in land use and settlement to a variety of environmental and cultural factors, including a change to substantially drier conditions. Archaeologists generally identify the beginning of the period with the appearance of the spear, atlatl, and milling or grinding tools and the end of the period with the appearance of pottery and horticulture. Although highly mobile, Archaic people exploited smaller and smaller territories over time as they increased their efforts to cultivate and harvest both wild plant resources and newly domesticated corn plants. Domesticated corn varieties were introduced into some Southwestern communities 3,000 to 5,000 years ago.

Associated sites typically consist of artifact scatters with hearths and other ash stains, remnants of brush structures, belowground storage pits, and late in the period shallow pit structures. In the Santa Fe area, early and middle Archaic sites occur on high terraces above Santa Fe River tributary floodplains, on canyon rims overlooking those drainages, and on elevated areas on the piedmont slopes between the foothills and grassland plains. Warm-season campsites are known in the higher foothills and mountains and on high ridges above streams and washes. Characteristic of the late Archaic are specialized hunting sites, quarries, and a variety of campsites with grinding tools in stream valleys, around springs, and in the piñon-juniper woodlands.

The **Developmental period** (A.D. 500/600 – 1175/1225) represents the beginning of what we identify as the Pueblo way of life. This period saw the introduction of the bow and arrow, the continued movement to lower elevations near agricultural lands, and a shift from isolated, belowground, straight-walled pit structures, to pit structures with aboveground jacal storage structures, to aboveground adobe pueblos of 10-12 rooms with pit structures.

Although groups during this period still relied on a wide variety of wild plant and animal resources, these wild foodstuffs assumed new supplementary roles as groups of people differentially incorporated agricultural staples of corn, beans and squash into their subsistence. Most archaeologists believe this subsistence shift was a response to changes in local demography, climate and resource availability, and group mobility. As group mobility became more restricted, these early Pueblo people occupied greater numbers of residential locations closer to water on a semiannual, if not year-round, basis. In the Santa Fe River valley, these sites dot the high terraces above the river.

Marking the **Coalition period** (A.D. 1175/1225 – 1300/1350) are three trends in population and settlement: substantial population growth and instability, expansion of permanent habitations into high elevation settings, and large increases in village size. Because the number and size of sites is so great, some archaeologists suggest area growth was a direct result of people leaving Chaco Canyon, the northern San Juan region, and Mesa Verde or from population pressure as in-coming groups prompted more and more movement across the larger region.

Groups increasingly settled narrow drainages within or at the base of mountain foothills, moving always closer to area floodplains. Later, some of these settlements became substantial year-round occupations centered on particular villages. This shift to upland settings presumably resulted from changing environmental conditions coupled with population pressure. Villages established at elevations higher than 6,000 ft encouraged Pueblo farmers to develop water-harvesting systems for producing crops in the region's cool, dry settings. Included for the first time in water harvesting techniques were water control features and rock-bordered grids for floodwater farming. Also occurring at this time were one- and two-room fieldhouses widely spaced across the landscape.

By the fourteenth century, populations were concentrated into a few large multi-roomblock settlements along both high and low portions of the Santa Fe River valley and its tributaries. Some archaeologists posit groups were moving between high and low elevation communities in response to local environmental changes or local social conditions. In part, this settlement shift also derived from changing precipitation patterns. Consistently above-average rainfall in the spring and early summer allowed farmers to intensify their agricultural pursuits by harvesting and conserving water for use by plants later in the summer, thus allowing the larger groupings of populations.

Besides proximity to surface water, **Classic period** (A.D. 1300/1350-1425/1450) settlements characteristically were near good agricultural land and in areas with favorable growing seasons. They also favored areas near extensive wood resources and ready access to abundant wild foods and raw material resources. The beginning of this period saw the initial appearance of multistoried towns of hundreds of rooms and several plazas. As was the case in earlier periods, these large-sized pueblos were not occupied continuously. People continued to build and use small villages in the surrounding areas.

Classic period farmers began developing diverse field systems based on harvesting and conserving water resources and expanding their use of wild plants and animals. Regardless of their efforts, agriculture proved unreliable over the long term in high-elevation settings where cooler temperatures decreased the number of frost-free days. Settlements were built, occupied and left within a generation or two, leaving only the largest and best-located communities. A number of these large consolidated communities occur within the Santa Fe River valley. Reasons provided by archaeologists for this realigning of settlements include the onset of cooler temperatures, population influxes, and competition over land and trade networks.

Pueblo oral histories tell a different story, however, explaining how the land must be given time to breathe and re-nourish itself. By leaving areas, they allowed the land to rest, but the intent always was to return to the remembered villages. This settlement pattern was one of Pueblo people cycling through areas, using and reusing areas, often changing that use to encourage an area's replenishment.

Fields in irrigation in the upper Canyon Road area, circa 1935.
Courtesy Palace of the Governors Photo Archive (NMHM/DCA). Negative No. 11125.

Looking Back, Looking Ahead

In Santa Fe we live in close proximity to our history. History surrounds us in the ancient adobe fabric of buildings and in place names that recall both those who founded Santa Fe and the native people who lived here before written history. There is an older history here too whose telling comes from native oral histories passed down through the generations, and from the many archaeological sites that dot the landscape in and around Santa Fe. Central to all these histories is the importance of land and water.

The archaeological record both complements and accentuates the many oral histories the different peoples of this region remember of their past, clearly illustrating the similarity of issues then and now. What guided native and historic peoples was a tradition of land and water use that recognized the essential relationship between a community and its hinterlands. This relationship defined, in part, their sense of place, their community, and to some degree their cultural identity. At every point in time, people made critical decisions about land, water, and community. Those decisions are visible in the types and distributions of settlements and activity areas remaining on the land; and in how individual groups defined and used geographical space, and most importantly, in how they defined their communities.

Histories told by Pueblo elders and Hispanic farmers and ranchers, who have lived on this land for many generations, and the archaeological investigations of the material remains left by their occupations provide us with an extraordinary record of the possibilities and the real limitations of the natural resources along the Santa Fe River. The archaeological record affords a telescopic view into the past, allowing us to review a range of adaptive strategies—some used successfully for long periods of time, and others cast off as innovations failed or new technologies developed. Perhaps now more than ever, the resources of the Santa Fe River are held in a delicate balance, poised between technology and a scale of intensive land use that can decimate this life-giving stream. Or, we can take steps to preserve for future generations this valuable resource that has sustained communities for thousands of years before us.

~~~

Cherie L. Scheick is the Program Director and owner of Southwest Archaeological Consultants in Santa Fe, and has been a practicing archaeologist for over 30 years. She is president of the not-for-profit Rio Grande Foundation for Communities and Cultural Landscapes. Ms. Scheick is actively involved in open space and community planning issues in Santa Fe, having served on city and county advisory groups and participated in a number of area master plans.

Dr. Frances Levine has been Director of the New Mexico History Museum since 2002 and has served as an expert witness on land and water use adjudications, utilizing her knowledge of historic settlement patterns, traditional land use, and cultural change. She is the author of numerous professional publications, including the books *Our Prayers Are in This Place: Pecos Pueblo Identity Over the Centuries* and *Surviving Extinction: The Legacy of Pecos Pueblo.*

Santa Fe River west of Castillo Street bridge, date unknown. Sylvia Loomis photograph collection. Courtesy of New Mexico State Records Center and Archives. Image No. 21990.

Santa Fe is at Last Supplied with Pure Mountain Water
The Mains Filled and Behaving in a Satisfactory Way
The Santa Fe New Mexican
April 1, 1882

The river's story might not have a beginning or an end, but the early 1880s saw significant changes that have determined its course for the last one hundred and thirty years. The damming of the river in 1881 would have tremendous impact on both the ecology and culture to which the river was central. While this jubilant article about the completion of the city's first municipal water supply encourages Santa Feans with the means to purchase water to do so, it doesn't ask what will be done by those who cannot afford it and are no longer are assured of "pure mountain water" flowing through the river.

It has now been considerably upwards of a year since the enterprise which had for its object the furnishing of Santa Fe with pure water from the mountains above the city, and the abolition of the practice of using water from wells in close proximity to sinks, was undertaken. The idea was a good one and the plan entirely feasible, although it made necessary a large amount of work and required a good deal of capital. It would have been completed long ago, but for certain financial difficulties which could not have been foreseen. These were finally overcome, and after some delay the work proceeded. The mains were laid through all the principal streets of the city, and up the cañon to a point at which it was best to locate the reservoir. A large dam was built across the cañon for the accumulation of water. This dam is situated at a much greater elevation than that of the city, thus giving a fall which will provide the necessary pressure. For several weeks past the works have been completed, but not until yesterday was everything in readiness for the turning on of water. Several lengths of defective pipes had been put in, causing leaks which it was necessary to repair. This gave rise to the impression that the plumbing had been poorly done, but Mr. Barbour informed the reporter that no such complaint could be made. He said that in hauling pipe, pieces had been apt to be cracked without the break being observed, and that this had happened at several instances, causing the trouble alluded to above. The leaks were stopped without trouble, and yesterday the water was turned on. The mains, it is estimated, hold altogether, including the city mains and the large one leading up to the dam, 170,000 gallons of water, and it took just an hour and a half to fill them, notwithstanding the heavy pressure there was no leakage except at the end of the main at Palace Avenue, and at the end of that on lower San Francisco Street. At these points the water burst forth for a time in considerable quantities, but was quickly stopped, and the pipes had been successfully filled and the enterprise proved in every way to be a success. As yet very few houses are supplied with water pipes, but now it is an assured fact that the water works will do what is promised. Many persons will proceed to provide for themselves the luxury of having water in their homes. The water furnished by the works is of the purest kind. It is soft, cold, and wholesome, and should be universally used. Aside from the convenience which patrons of the works will enjoy, the question of health is sufficient to induce every homeowner in Santa Fe who can possibly do so to become a water taker. There are few wells in the city whose waters are not impure on account of sewage from sinks, and physicians pronounce the water in many instances injurious to health. With all these advantages the city water cannot fail to become popular and generally used throughout the city. Take it and be healthy, while at the same time you encourage an enterprise which deserves well at the hands of the people of Santa Fe.

Letter to the Acequia Association
From the Santa Fe Water Company

In 1893 a second, larger dam was built on the Santa Fe River and the supply of water to acequias dried up while it filled. In this letter the Santa Fe Water Company acknowledges the needs and rights of frustrated local farmers and attempts to relieve their concerns. Though this letter makes promises to the contrary, by mid-summer even irrigation from the pipes had been cut off "on account of imminent danger of water famine" (The Santa Fe New Mexican, July 5 1893). A water sharing agreement was later worked out.

March 14, 1893

To the people of la Acequia known as la Acequia del Cerro Gordo, in the County of Santa Fe, New Mexico:

The Water and Improvement Company wishes to advise you that it has obtained from the County and by purchase of individuals the right of all surplus water in the Santa Fe River; this is all the water that is not necessary for the use of all persons under old Acequias as yours. That the present work they are doing now is not with the purpose of interfering with your Acequias and although the dam of your Acequia has been cut the company proposes and will supply your Acequia with enough water for your use by means of pipe lines and pipes until the present work is finished when all the water of the River less sufficient to fill the tank of the dam will run by the tunnel to the south side of the river and will be delivered to the Acequia belonging to you and to the other Acequias under the direction of the Mayordomos as has been done in the past, and all expense incurred with the change will be defrayed by the Company. The quantity of water supplies from the river to the Acequias will not be lessened, only the manner of taking the same will be changed, and it is believed that in such manner as shall be more satisfactory to you, this company wishes to act always in harmony with you and with all others to have rights in Acequias and will always work together with you with the purpose to make the water reach in all possible ways to all persons entitled to the same and with as less cost as possible.

Respectfully,
L.A. Hughes
President of the Water and Improvement Company
Translated from the Spanish by the County Clerk's Office

Memorias del Río

Melinda Romero Pike

From the beginning of time, the spirit of man has found comfort, serenity, and security in the life giving waters of a river. As we know, the Santa Fe River is no exception. The river was the determining factor in the colonizing of Santa Fe.

I grew up playing on the sandy bank of the Santa Fe River in the Village of Agua Fria. We children built sand castles, digging holes with our bare hands in the sand, experiencing the joy of seeing the water gush upward. The giant cottonwood *bosques*, more than 100 years old, were the ideal environment for children to bond with the beauty of nature. In those meadows and *jarrales* (willow thickets) we could play, dream, and be creative.

As children, it was pleasant waking up to the sounds and scents of the river. Not the aroma of Juan Valdez' coffee, but the smell of sweet wet sand. As nighttime fell, all we heard were the echoing sounds of water flowing on its journey to meet the Rio Grande in unison with the orchestrated sounds of crickets and frogs.

Regrettably, all of this is extinct. In the 1880s, a group of men incorporated the Santa Fe Water and Improvement Company to build reservoirs for the storage of water. The water from the reservoirs would be diverted through large pipes to supply the city.

The blockage of the river's flow was the beginning of the death of the river. The residents downstream were confronted with calamities that created many hardships for the survival of their families and their animals. After the water ceased flowing, the people resorted to dry farming and more favors were expected from Patron "San Isidro." Remember that these were people of Great Faith who celebrated the little occasional flow from the river.

These people only wanted to live in peace and raise their families. They were only trying to survive. The residents knew that they were holders of irrevocable water rights. In 1896 they petitioned to the highest authority, the sitting Governor of the Territory of New Mexico, but their voices went unheard. As if that wasn't enough, they were not compensated for the rights that were unjustly snatched from them. Here is their petition—the words of my ancestors translated from the Spanish by my son, Steven Pike MD, JD.

Your Excellency W.T. Thornton, Governor of New Mexico:

We, petitioners, residents of Santa Fe County Precinct No. 5 who have signed below, owners of various properties and heads of families, respectfully present to your Excellency that we have been unjustly deprived of our Santa Fe River water rights by the Santa Fe Water Company. Many of our families, our animals, and we petitioners are suffering greatly because the Santa Fe Water Company is diverting the Santa Fe River water that we have had an irrevocable privilege to use since our ancestors' time. As of the present date we still have not been able to plant our crops for lack of water; crops that we depend on to support our families.

For these reasons, to your Excellency, the Executive of the New Mexico Territory, we ask that you take the necessary steps that are just and proper to ensure that our water rights are respected and that you grant our plea, otherwise our families will perish of hunger because we cannot plant our crops for lack of water. Observing that solely we the inhabitants of said Precinct No. 5 know the severity of the present calamity, and that as of this date we have not been able to get one solitary drop of water for our crops nor one solitary drop of water for our animals,

We Petitioners
Continue Pleading to You

1. Jose Montoya
2. Encarnacion Ribal
3. Lino Montoya
4. Eloisa Lopez
5. Pablo Ortiz
6. Refugio Romero
7. Carlos Ortiz
8. Manuelita Romero
9. Bonifacio Rivera
10. Juanita Ortiz
11. Delwina Gallegos
12. Jose Montoya
13. Isabel Gallegos
14. Emiterio Ribera
15. Ignasito Lopez
16. Pedro Varela
17. Ambrichita Gonzales
18. Cirvais Baca
19. Ignacia Baca
20. Ascencion Romero
21. Juanita Baca
22. Manuelita Rael
23. Amiseta Rael
24. Felipe Trujillo
25. Salome Rael
26. Condelario Gonzales
27. Juanita Sena
28. Jose Antonio Montoya
29. Gertrudes Mora
30. Abran Erera
31. Rufina Montoya
32. Camilo Erera
33. Juan La Romero
34. Agafrito Erera
35. Sifriana Lusero
36. Vecolas Lopez
37. Sabinita Tafoya
38. Juan Lopez
39. Petra Martínez
40. Antonio Mora
41. Foroseno Gurule
42. Isabel Erera
43. Felisiana Martin
44. Francisco Carillo
45. Selestino Romero

46. Petrolina Ernandes
47. Juan Gonsales
48. Juanita Romero
49. Miguel Carillo
50. Simona Bustamante
51. Tibursio Lopes
52. Juanita Montoya
53. Longino Tafoya
54. Candelario Baca
55. Pablo Gonsalez
56. Tomastina Gonsalez
57. Jose Padia
58. Juanita Baca

59. Manuel Gonsalez
60. Condelario Romero
61. Tomita Lopez
62. Dolores Lopez
63. Petra Montoya
64. Fabian Lopez
65. Margarita Tafoya
66. Ysidro Lopez
67. Tonita Montoya
68. Bisente Camilla
69. Plasida Lopez

And 97 Dependents

Orchard and garden in foreground, DeVargas Street and tree lined Santa Fe River in background, date unknown. Frank McNitt Photograph Collection. Courtesy New Mexico State Records Center and Archives. Image No. 6864.

This was not the first time that a request for water would be made to the highest legal authorities of New Mexico, nor would it be the last. During the drought of 1885, local farmers and residents submitted a petition to the Territorial Legislature in an effort to save some of their water. The petition counted 560 signatures and was signed by two Mayordomos de Agua, Albino Ortega and Cipriano Chavez. They stated that all the river water was being held in the reservoirs, its release blocked by the Water Company. The following is translated from their petition: "The great majority of the people in Santa Fe have always lived from agriculture producing huge crops, but to date this has been reduced more and more by being deprived of our water rights by millionaire companies."

The newcomers that came to govern the newly acquired territory had little respect or regard for the people already living here. The original Santa Feans could trace their presence here to the late 16 and early 1700s. Despite their long history, they often felt intimidated because the new American laws were unfamiliar to them. They wanted to respect and abide by the law, but because of the language barrier they couldn't always understand it. Sadly, the Americans didn't have the same respect for the laws that had governed water use in New Mexico for centuries. They violated the law of prior appropriation. The unlawful upstream diversion and taking of water by junior water users violated the seniority rights of the downstream users. The downstream users never forfeited nor abandoned their pre-1907 senior water rights. Those rights were unjustly taken without compensation and even now unfair tactics have been employed in the *Anaya v. PNM* Santa Fe River Basin water adjudication to deny restitution to the Agua Fria people of their senior rights.

Much of these injustices and broken promises were a direct consequence of the policy of the United States government and its leaders to follow the "Doctrine of Discovery" sometimes also stated in law books as the "Doctrine of Conquest." The Doctrine of Discovery was a way for conquering nations to legitimize their oppression of the conquered. For example, that Doctrine (not recognized as a legitimate doctrine of law for many decades) justified the taking of indigenous people's property, denying them human rights, and generally treating them as "heathens" that needed to be "saved" and converted to western values and beliefs. That Doctrine nearly eliminated Native American culture and in New Mexico justified violating treaties, denying equal application of law to Hispanics, unlawful taking of properties, and water rights, and other injustices. Many times the United States Courts were used to "sanitize" those violations, as judicial decisions often would uphold the human rights violations. In recent years, many of those historical wrongs have been gradually overturned by Supreme Courts and International Courts all over the world. But even the Supreme Court in this country was a party to "legitimizing" the injustices.

Pleas and grievances like the ones quoted above are numerous and very painful. One of the most devastating things was when the petitioners walked down the Santa Fe streets and saw the magnificent gardens with the beautiful

"*Pilas de Cantera*" fountains shooting spurts of water up in the air and displaying entertaining forms. This was in stark contrast to the plight of people who were clamoring for a small portion of water for domestic use and drinking water for their domestic animals. Only people with "Hearts of Stone" would not have empathy for such a situation.

It was also difficult for the people to fathom how the river's flow was now converted to an underground system flowing through large pipes and leaving the river bone dry. All this altered and defied nature. With the absence of water in the channel, the riverbed has endured many transgressions. In addition to my wonderful memories of the river, I have painful ones of the huge crusher situated on the riverbed just a short distance from my house and the giant dump trucks hauling sand and gravel day in and day out. All the sand and gravel that was needed for the developments of Casa Alegre and Casa Solana came directly from the Santa Fe River. In the days when no restrictions existed, the riverbed was the perfect site to unload big blocks of concrete and other trash from construction projects. Sewage spills and other pollutants further contaminated the river. So much mining and dumping in the river altered the natural meander of the river. The channel became very deep and the banks eroded.

Fishing on the upper Santa Fe River, date unknown. Courtesy Palace of the Governors Photo Archive (NMHM/DCA). Negative No. 61587.

Thank God for the new regulations that exist today for the restoration of healthy rivers, which in turn protects the aquifer and hopefully, our health as consumers of water. The people whose lives were forever changed by the theft of their water cannot be compensated for what they lost. The injustices of the past can never be completely repaired. But the water belongs to the river, and should be allowed to flow for the sake of our aquifers and the riparian areas along the river. It should flow for the benefit of all.

My hope for the return of water in the river will never die. The late Mr. Antonio Montoya shared this hope. When he passed away in 1995 at age 95, he was the oldest resident of Agua Fria. I am confident his memories of the river were even more memorable than mine, of a time when the acequias flowed to capacity carrying the life sustaining water for fields, orchards, animals, fish, and the natural vegetation. He too longed for the river to again become viable, flowing with life giving water. "Even," he said, "if it is just a trickle."

Kudos to Mayor David Coss and all the friends of the River, its Commission, the Santa Fe Watershed Association, and ¡YouthWorks! for having the will and hope to heal and give life back to the river. The river thirsts and is pleading with us for:

"UN CHORRO DE AGUA POR FAVOR"

~~~~

For decades, Santa Fe Living Treasure Melinda Romero Pike has carried the river's stories, tirelessly telling them to ensure that the once-living river's history is never forgotten. Ms. Pike was a member of the River Task Force in the 1990's and currently serves on the Santa Fe River Commission.

THE WATER QUESTION
The City of Santa Fe Naturally Entitled to First and Full Use of Supply
MAYORDOMOS INSIST On Appropriating Entire
Flow Regardless of the Town's Necessities and Rights
The Santa Fe New Mexican
June 1, 1904

In the spring of 1904, a combination of drought and impoundment dried up the acequias once again. Mayordomos Petronillo Armijo, Francisco Gonzales y Chavez, and Simon Segura went to the Santa Fe Water Company to request that water from the reservoir be released to the ditches. On May 26ᵗʰ The Santa Fe New Mexican reported that, "The water company in view of straits of people represented by the mayordomos agreed to give them water for irrigation Monday and assured them that if rain fell and storm waters could be preserved that they would be allowed an allotment of it as a matter of grace and courtesy." The rain must not have come. When this headline appeared a week later, the hostile tone and inflammatory language indicate that tensions had risen considerably.

There are three overseers of ditches or mayordomos of acequias, as they are known in the limpid Spanish language in the city precincts. These powerful officials are of the opinion and have proclaimed that the entire water supply of this town of 7,500 to 8,000 people is theirs for the irrigation of a few corn patches and that all the water flow of the Santa Fe River is to be disposed of by them regardless of the rights, privileges, and immunities of the thousands of inhabitants of this town. These three men care very little for the good or ill of the city, but they say that they must have the water supply of the river, all of it, or there will be trouble. The question at the bottom of this is simple. Do the rights, privileges, and necessities of the inhabitants of this city govern or do the arbitrary will and say so of the three mayordomos carry the day? These three "grandees" have informed the management of the Santa Fe Water and Light Company that all of this water supply is theirs to be done with as their own free, sweet will and personal interest dictate and that they will have it, regardless of the absolute necessity and requirements of the city in the shape of water for domestic use and a supply in case of fire. Manager Frank Owen of the Water Company, however, considers that the good of the city is to be first observed by the company and hence will not allow the mayordomos to carry out their designs.

Last Monday at a consultation between Mr. Owen and these water bosses, he told them that he might be willing if the circumstances and the water flow would allow to give them part of the water for irrigation purposes. This partial offer was scornfully rejected and the water bosses insisted on everything in the water line or the heavy hand of the law would be invoked and brought down with smashing force on the water company as well as on the city. The manager of the Water Company could but shrug his shoulders and tell these high, mighty and potent bosses to go ahead.

For many years past there has been more or less trouble over this water question and it is about time that it were settled. There is no question but that all original water rights accrued to the inhabitants of the city of Santa Fe primarily. From the first day of settlement all the water that was necessary for the support and maintenance of the town was appropriated by it and for the use and benefit of its citizens. Ditches and acequias that were taken out afterwards for the purpose of irrigation could in the very nature of things only use the water supply not needed for the town or city itself.

For the past eleven months a very severe drouth has obtained in this section and the water supply is naturally very short. The principles of the greatest good for the greatest number and public policy must govern. The citizens and inhabitants of Santa Fe must stand by the contentions and claims of the Santa Fe Water and Light Company that all the water necessary for the city must be preserved in the Company's reservoir and if thereafter there be any surplus, that might be turned over to the mayordomos of acequias for use in the ditches. It is also plain that no matter what amount of water is given these mayordomos now, irrigation can do but little good as it is too late in the season and as the small crops raised in the vicinity of town and under these ditches cannot be saved this year.

At this writing it is not yet known what measures the mayordomos have taken. The Water Company is ready and willing to do all it can to have an amicable settlement of this matter, but it is bound under its contract and charter to provide the necessary water supply for the city for domestic uses and increase fire at all hazards and as complete as possible.

It would certainly be criminal folly to sacrifice the necessities and interests of this city to the domineering will and bullheadedness of these mayordomos and for the sake allowing a few persons to raise two or three hundred dollars worth of corn and vegetables.

Santa Fe River Chronicle: A History of the Last 400 Years

Tara M. Plewa

Introduction and Setting

*I*n northern New Mexico around 1605, Spanish settlers began selecting a site for the villa that would later become the modern-day City of Santa Fe. Tree-ring data reveal the decade of settlement to be one of the wettest in the last five hundred years. During that time, water filled the Santa Fe River. It flowed steeply and freely from high in the watershed, exiting the metamorphic rocks of the Sangre de Cristo Mountains, and meandering through high terraces of gravel and sand into the valley below. There, the river would begin to braid in pattern, and widen in the area known today as downtown Santa Fe: an adjustment in planform in response to the stark change in slope, and the large volume of sediment it was carrying.

The river continued to change position, or laterally migrate over the years as it flowed through its wide, sandy floodplain until reaching La Bajada canyon. Upon entering the gorge it had cut over thousands of years, the river's ability to meander is lessened because of its confinement between steep walls of thick basaltic rock. Until modern times, the Santa Fe River exited the gorge and wound through a grassy plain before joining the Rio Grande near Cochiti Pueblo. Before the influence of humans, the Santa Fe River would likely flow continuously in the wettest years from its origin in Lake Peak high in the watershed, to its relative terminus at its confluence with the Rio Grande. Seasonal and climatic fluctuations aside, the occurrence of water along its entire course is undeniable, given the citations found in early documents, the presence of long-abandoned pueblos along its course, and the early farms that dot its corridor, with names all indicative of the continued presence of water: Cieneguita (near present-day Frenchy's Field), Agua Fria, Cienega Grande (present day La Cienega), and Cieneguilla. Even the place name of the ruined pueblo that once housed Native Americans north of the river, Kaupoge, means "place of shell beads by the water" and bolsters the argument for a long history of continuous flow.

The Governor of New Mexico, Pedro de Peralta, approved of the villa's location for its water abundance, its favorable farming conditions, its lack of Indian occupants, and its similarities to the ideal New World settlement site described in a 1573 royal decree, *Recopilación de Leyes de los Reynos de las Indias* (Laws of the Indies). The river was flanked by a *bosque* (forested floodplain), wide and flat river terraces ideal for farming, and a nearby *cienega* (marshland) later used as a community-owned pasture for animal husbandry and hay cultivation for royal livestock. During those wet years early in the history of settlement, there was ample water for the small population of several hundred; enough for *acequia* (irrigated) agriculture, livestock watering, milling, and adobe construction.

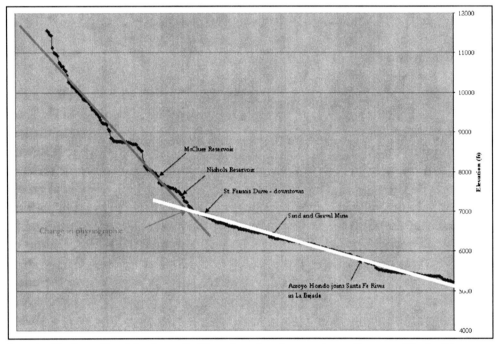

Longitudinal profile of the Santa Fe River from headwaters to confluence with the Rio Grande. Courtesy Tara Plewa.

However, despite first impressions, Peralta's site choice was dangerous for several reasons. In the villa's precarious position it was made to feel the wrath of seasonal flooding, to suffer the effects of poor drainage, and to fight a continued battle against the river and its tendency to redirect its primary course into the heart of the settlement: into a small side-channel dubbed the *Rio Chiquito*, a path now occupied by modern-day Water Street. The river naturally meanders through the valley to dissipate energy and without human interference would, over time, have occupied the Rio Chiquito by converting this side stream to its main thread. Evidence of its movement is indicated by both river sediments deposited in the terraces paralleling its course, and the subtle changes in elevation revealed by Geographic Information System modeling. Peralta could not have chosen a poorer position for the villa from the perspective of river flooding. There was no protection from the stupendous floods that likely came raging down the valley each spring. Torrents of debris-choked waters undoubtedly destroyed many adobe homes and other man-made infrastructure. The first newspaper of Santa Fe tells many tales of floods and their toll upon the town, as reports of bridge washouts are ample in these written records. The saturated subsurface from springs, the roots from trees in the bosque, the local cienega, and the water applied via irrigated agriculture aided in the permanency of the Santa Fe River's position, as wet sands and gravels supported by the roots of vegetation are more stable and less easily eroded than dry, un-vegetated areas.

Acequia construction began immediately upon arrival at the site so that fields of beans, corn, and hay would produce in their first year. The land was divided amongst settlers, and the long-established Spanish traditions of acequia agriculture were applied to the lands of Santa Fe. Acequias are hand-dug, unlined irrigation ditches that carry water under the force of gravity into the fields flanking the river. Water in the river is diverted into *Acequia Madres* (main ditches) through the manipulation of *compuertas* (gates*)*, and after potentially traveling a half-dozen miles, and changing direction several times, it moves through laterals and *sangrias* (smaller ditches), and finally reaches the *milpas* (fields). Once the water enters a field and is spread across the landscape under gravity, the farmer helps the water reach all the furrows and the farthest corners by moving clods of dirt with his shovel. The word *acequia* refers not only to the ditch, but also to the community that relies upon it. Acequia community rules for water division, application, and ditch maintenance stem from Roman and Moorish influences, and apply to each farmer and their families.

Acequia farmer passing on the ancient oral tradition, circa 1940. Courtesy of Palace of the Governors Photo Archive, (NMHM/DCA). Negative No. 58868.

In recent times, the Office of the State Engineer has determined that the average application rate for water to Santa Fe fields each growing season is 4.5 acre-feet per acre. One acre-foot is equal to the volume of water it takes to cover one square acre of land with one foot of water. By applying this factor to the acres of arable land in Santa Fe, as gathered from historical maps and aerial photography at different snapshots in time, average water withdrawals from the Santa Fe River are known. Comparing the withdrawal rates with the timing of wet and dry periods from climate research, and while considering the changing needs of humans within the watershed, the importance of water in the context of Santa Fe history is revealed. Water in the river, either its presence or its absence, explains a great deal about the struggles for survival at *La Villa Real de la Santa Fé de San Francisco de Asís*.

Early River Patterns

Water was available during the growing season in a pattern that would become recognizable over the years. As the large winter snowpack began to melt, the river would bulge beyond its banks. Early in its history, the villa's buildings were far enough from the river to avoid the average overbank flows, so damage to early human infrastructure was small. At the beginning of the seasonal surge, harvestable waters were diverted into the acequias, and planting began. Early river manipulations by humans were small, consisting mainly of small berms of earth heaped into the channel to divert some of its water into the nearby ditch. As the winter snowpack began to subside, the river's meltwaters were supplemented by summer rainstorms, or Monsoons. During the Monsoons, torrential downpours would flood the river and commonly cause it to leave its banks. Despite the harsh, unpredictable conditions, within a few years the settlement had acequias and fields filling the valley.

Around 1620, the climate began to change and water availability went from a time of plenty to a time of want. These cycles of wet and dry continued for decades, with the 1666-1672 period being so extendedly dry that irrigated agriculture could not sustain the local population, and the Mission Supply Service imported food into Santa Fe. Through these early decades, the increasing population (1,100 by 1630) put pressure on the local water resources, and a lack of river water meant a subsequent lack of food for the populace. Land up and down the valley had been converted to agriculture, which meant less water for more fields, and as a result, arguments over water allocations erupted. The drought also put pressure on the local Native American communities, and stoked the fires for the ensuing Pueblo Revolt of 1680. During the revolt, water played a pivotal role in Santa Fe's downfall. The main acequia to the *casas reales* (royal compound) was severed by the invaders, who cut off the water supply to the entire population walled-up inside. After three days without water, the settlers and their remaining livestock fled the villa.

Twelve years later, when the villa and surrounding lands were reclaimed for Spain, a well was dug inside the compound to ensure that a lack of water would never cost the villa again. During reestablishment, and for decades following, Santa Fe River water continued on its seasonal cycles, with larger regional climate fluctuations causing droughts and floods through the years. There are only a few remaining documents that describe the condition of the Santa Fe River prior to the arrival of the newspaper to Santa Fe in 1847. The documented flood of October 16th, 1767 is one of these examples, and describes a potential one-hundred-year flood event that cut into the Rio Chiquito, making it deeper and wider as the river tried to change the position of its main channel. One of the earliest surviving documents that pertain directly to the Santa Fe River is this call to action by Governor Pedro Fermin de Mendinueta. This document reveals details about the massive flood, and the earliest known major construction initiative on the Santa Fe River. Physical evidence of this event is long-gone; however, a description of the havoc it wreaked is so severe that every resident of the villa was required to dedicate labor to its restoration. The document describes the:

> Threat the river of this villa is to the churches, royal houses and others in the center of this villa, by its unusual crest the 16th and 17th of this past October, filling its ancient bed with stones and sand, for which reason its current took it into that which is called the Rio Chiquito, causing considerable damage to the houses and farm lands; … timbers be brought to be placed in the weakest spots that they might serve as footings and support for [against] the stone and sand where the river might leave its former bed, in order that it maintain its usual current; and in order that the projected and necessary work be done and carried to the desired effect, I order by this public decree that all citizens and soldiers of this villa and fort, with the exception of no one, heed the above stated work with whatever pertains to each the most equitable consideration and methods.

At the time, it was important that the river remain in its original course, because a permanent change in its location would put the royal buildings in greater danger from flow events due to their new proximity to the channel. It is likely that Santa Feans tried several methods to protect their homes and churches from the river, like creating levees. Photography from the late 1800s shows material on either side of the river that appears shaped like artificial levees, keeping water from flooding the center of the villa. Other historic photography shows the bridges as causeways above the river course: their average spans giving clues to channel widths during larger flow events. Physical evidence of these early earthen control structures no longer exists today, having been obliterated by modern infrastructure.

First page of Governor's order for river restoration after 1767 flood. Pinart/Bancroft Collection: P-E 53:5. Courtesy of the Bancroft Library, University of California, Berkeley.

The earliest surviving depiction of Santa Fe comes from Urrutia in 1768; his map details the location of the post-Revolt *casas reales*, the surrounding fields, the Santa Fe River, and a possible lateral acequia. Urrutia's portrayal shows a gravelly floodplain; an early characteristic of this river that was the result of large deposits of sand and gravel that it entrains as it flows through the upper watershed, and later deposits downstream. By 1776, despite the supplemental waters of local springs, the carrying capacity of the river had been reached. There were more fields in irrigation than available water to support them. With an average application rate of 4.5 acre-feet of water per acre, there simply was not enough to be divided amongst everyone. Based on the last 93 years of river flow data, the average water yield from the upstream watershed during the growing season is 36 acre-feet per day and can provide enough water to support approximately 2,000 acres each growing season. Fields and ditches extended up and down the Santa Fe River valley: upstream beyond the modern-day dams, and downstream beyond Agua Fria and the current wastewater treatment plant, far exceeding the 2,000-acre threshold.

Wide floodplain of the Santa Fe River above Galisteo Street, date unknown. Courtesy of Palace of the Governors Photo Archive (NMHM/DCA). Negative No. 61570.

By irrigating land flanking the river, the character of the Santa Fe River changed over time. One hundred and fifty years of water application to the fields had saturated the subsurface. The materials beneath Santa Fe are sands and gravels from Pleistocene glacial outwash, which conduct water efficiently. Despite evaporation and crop use, trillions of gallons of water were applied to the valley floor each year. A great deal percolated, entered the groundwater, and fed the river. Geologists Spiegel and Baldwin (1963) suggest that approximately 30 to 50 percent of water spread onto the land for irrigation contributed to river flow via groundwater recharge. This extensive water application and field spreading played a pivotal role in shaping the physical and cultural landscape of the valley, and explain a great deal about Santa Fe hydrology. The valley floor was considerably wetter than would have existed under non-irrigated conditions, and the additional river flow created a system of continuous feedback, allowing farmers to ultimately convert even more land to agriculture.

Comparison of Urrutia map of 1768, left, with modern Santa Fe.

Governmental Changes Cause River Repercussions

The coming of US Territoriality brought both physical and cultural changes to the landscape. In the Kearny Code, laws written for the new territory specified that no acequias were to be disturbed, and that water rights were to remain intact. US laws placed governance on the counties however, and because Santa Fe went unincorporated until 1892, all decisions for the villa were made by county commissioners. In 1870, the commissioners of Santa Fe County gave the rights to build dams, impound and distribute water, and create electricity to the Santa Fe Water and Improvement Company. Old Stone Dam was the first impoundment constructed on the Santa Fe River in 1880, and held a mere 25 acre-feet of water (8 million gallons). The volume of water in the Santa Fe River each year averages 5,500 acre-feet (1.8 trillion gallons), and because the dam was so small, the effects on river hydrology were limited once the reservoir had filled. Deemed too small for the growing town, a second dam (Two-Mile) was constructed 1,500 feet downstream of Old Stone in 1893. This dam held 387 acre-feet (126 million gallons), was significantly larger, and could impound seven percent of the river's total annual flow. Immediate changes were noticed downstream, both in the river's physical character and in the acequias, while above the dams, the river flowed as it had until reaching the reservoir pool. The river's hydrologic regime upstream from the dams, including variations in magnitude, duration, timing, frequency and rate of change of water flow events, continued to respond to the local climatic inputs, such as seasonal snow melt. Beaver still built lodges in the channel, creating small areas of ponding, wildlife habitat, and groundwater recharge. Downstream, however, the river's physical character and hydrologic regime became significantly different.

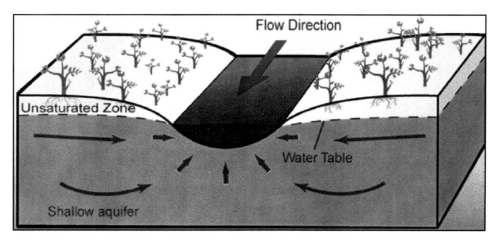

Understanding subsurface flow. Streams gain water from inflow of groundwater through the streambed. Illustration from "Groundwater and Surface Water a Single Resource" by TC Winter, WH Judson, OL Franke, and WM Alley. Circular 1139, U.S. Geological Survey, Denver.

The Santa Fe River Downstream from Dams

Dams introduce an artificial terminus into a gradually sloping river. Dams collect the water behind them for later release, and have several purposes. In Santa Fe, dams currently provide 40 percent of the city's water supply needs, flood control, and a source of water for fire protection in the city and upper watershed. The river's velocity drops drastically when it encounters the reservoir, and so does its ability to carry sediment. Any sediment in the water drops out at the beginning of the reservoir pool. Below the dam, the character of flow changes to reflect the conditions induced by dam operations, including significant decreases in the average volume of water in the river, the timing of the flows (seasonality), and reductions in the magnitude and duration of the flow events. The river pursues dynamic equilibrium by trying to reestablish its sediment load after the dam's filtering effect. The lack of sediment in the water below the dam causes the river to cut down into its bed by first picking up sediment in sizes that it has the energy to carry, mostly the finer materials, like sands, silts and gravels. Materials of smaller size were removed from the river's bed first, and then from its banks. When the dams were first constructed, the effects on the downstream morphology were expressed in downcutting, evident in paired photography. Downstream residents in Agua Fria used to train their horses in the finer sands of the dry channel before the weaker river washed away this smaller sediment size.

Downtown Santa Fe River ca. 1910   Downtown Santa Fe River ca. 1914

Paired photography showing downstream incision as a result of dams. Picture on left shows downtown Santa Fe River in 1910, picture on right is the same location in 1914. Courtesy Palace of the Governors Photo Archives (NMHM/DCA). Negative No.'s 61466 and 11051.

The Santa Fe River below the dam has minimal stream power however (reduced energy to entrain and carry sediment), and the small volume of water that is released by the dams is not powerful enough to mobilize the riverbed, creating an armored condition. The river simply does not have enough energy to pick up and carry the boulders that line its bottom.

The citizens of Santa Fe saw the changes in the river's banks, and tried to stabilize them. The banks of the river at the Galisteo Street Bridge were reinforced with posts driven into the ground, horizontal timbers, brush and stacked stone, giving us a glimpse of the early riverworks fashioned to control channel position in downtown. The Civilian Conservation Corps constructed more stable walls of concrete and stone to contain the river flows, and protect the banks from lateral cutting. Over a period of a few decades, the river changed from a braided stream with large volumes of sediment, and seasonal waters to a narrow, single-thread stream without a sediment source or a reliable water supply. Aside from spring dam releases that occur when the reservoirs have reached their capacity, seasonal flows are held behind the reservoir, and there was very little water in the river for the acequias. If it was a dry year, all water was held behind the dams to ensure the public water supply was maintained.

The flood of 1904 proved the "staunchness" of the new reservoirs, and showed their ability to protect the villa from the floods that had endangered them for centuries. For three hundred years, the upper watershed had been used intensively for community grazing and logging, and as a result, the vegetation was sparse and exposed sediment was easily mobilized by summer Monsoons. On Thursday evening, September 29, a thunderstorm sent sediment-laden floodwaters writhing down the narrow mountain stream course, frothing with rock, sand and debris, and upon reaching the first reservoir, was immediately slowed by the reduction in slope, the widening channel, and the pool of Old-Stone dam, and thus began to settle. The reservoir immediately filled with sediment, and Two-Mile Dam succeeded in holding the major floodwaters at bay. *The New Mexican* reported on Saturday, October 1, that "if the crest of the flood had struck Santa Fe, the entire lower portion of the town would undoubtedly have been inundated and many buildings washed out."

As the seriousness of the flood sank in, so did the realization that the dam had saved the town. The gravity of the potential damage raised awareness of the condition of the upper watershed, and how proper management was critical to maintaining the population's major water source. As a result, the upper watershed was closed to all human entrants by the US Department of Agriculture in 1932 to protect it from fire, erosion, and pollution. To better understand the variations in stream flow, the US Geologic Survey installed a stream gaging station above the reservoirs on the Santa Fe River in 1913. This device measures the amount of water in the stream, and generates data used to compare seasonal and annual trends, and the hydrologic effects of Nichols Dam later constructed above the gage.

Large-Scale Impacts of Humans Within the Watershed

As the local population quadrupled from 5,072 in 1910 to over 20,000 by the end of the 1930s, so did the pressure on local water resources. Ironically, this period is one of the wettest in the last five hundred years, perhaps giving the local populace false hope about future water availability in northern New Mexico. The water company responded to the population surge by constructing Granite Point Dam in 1926 (later renamed McClure). The original structure could hold 650 acre-feet of water, and increased Santa Fe's total available storage behind dams to 1,035 acre-feet (337 million gallons), a volume equivalent to approximately 19 percent of the river's annual flow. With these two structures in place, the acequias received very little, if any water at all. Spring snowmelt was retained behind the dams, and only after the reservoirs were full would water enter the river. Granite

Point was raised less than a decade later to deal with the surge in population, and when completed in 1935, could hold 3,059 acre-feet (997 million gallons). Now, over 60 percent of the river's average annual flow was being stored. Nichols Dam was constructed above Two-Mile reservoir in 1943, and added 684 acre-feet (223 million gallons) to Santa Fe's total water storage.

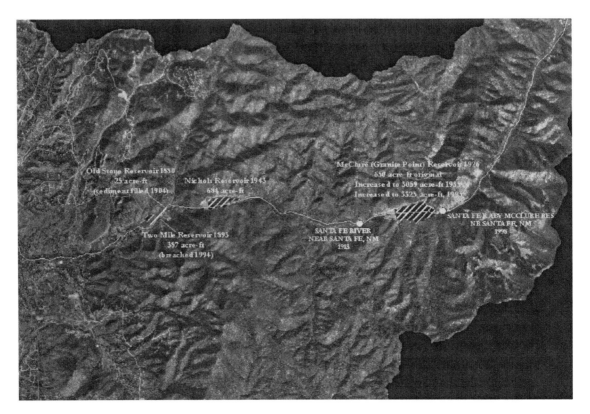

Reservoir location map with stream gages. Courtesy Tara Plewa.

The downstream effects of the dams were immediate. Combined, these structures had the ability to withhold approximately 75 percent of the river's annual flow at one time. With the local population using the river's waters as their daily supply, the reservoirs captured all incoming water as quickly as it was used. As a result, acequia agriculture in Santa Fe virtually stopped. At the time, World War II began calling all able-bodied men away from the villa and when they returned, instead of farming, they sought other jobs in manufacturing and other sectors. With no water in the river, both the physical and cultural landscapes of Santa Fe changed dramatically.

The drought of the 1950s brought three significant changes to the hydrology of Santa Fe. First, the amount of land in irrigation declined significantly as a result of increasing reservoir storage from 1,200 acres in 1917 to approximately 650 acres in 1951. Second, acequia agriculture losses directly influenced the amount of water in the river by removing an important source of subsurface flow. Two major sources of river water were unavailable for irrigating: upper watershed flow due to drought, and subsurface flow contributions from agriculture. Third, the City of Santa Fe drilled wells along the river in 1946, and 1950, and thus large-scale pumping for public water supply began; withdrawals creating cones of depression and changing the direction of groundwater flow. The Santa Fe River was a gaining stream for centuries until modern pumping began. With these three changes happening in concert, the physical effects on the river were significant.

Within twenty years, the river channel narrowed by tens of feet. Walls constructed to protect the riverbanks from erosion have forced a formerly meandering system to run swiftly through a straight chute, and have focused the river's energy onto its bed. As a result, the formerly cohesive substrate of sands and gravels, held together by a high water table and the roots of vegetation, was easily cut and incision began. The rivercourse narrowed and deepened over the years. A deeper channel allowed for floods to be contained within it, and as land values in downtown Santa Fe grew, so did the ability to develop the parcels adjacent to the river.

Downstream below Agua Fria, sand and gravel mines began taking large volumes of sediment from the riverbed. This practice remained unchecked for decades, and as a result, serious problems with the physical form of the river materialized in headward erosion. The sand and gravel mines created an abrupt change in river slope by removing millions of tons of material from specific points along the channel. The river adjusted to this removal by redistributing sediment within the floodplain and cutting in the upstream direction. The scars of this process are still evident today because the river is still adjusting, and cutting in concert. Current river restoration efforts below Agua Fria will continue to battle the effects of headward erosion until the mining of sand and gravel from the Santa Fe River is stopped.

Despite the presence of upstream dams, floods still threaten downtown Santa Fe. Once roads were paved, stormwater was directed into the Santa Fe River via curb inlets. As development expanded in the watershed, so did the volume of runoff entering the river, and today, the river acts as a giant storm drain for the city. A serious flooding event in 1966, recorded in *The New Mexican*, illustrates that despite upstream flood control, the capacity for large storms to cause serious infrastructural damage to downtown Santa Fe increases as development spreads. Creating stormwater detention opportunities, however small, are essential to the success of the different restoration efforts currently underway on the river.

River Awareness and Restoration Efforts

In 1980, the first written river plan called attention to the stream's degraded condition and offered a few suggestions for changes in the downtown area.

Although the suggestions were not implemented, other modifications to water management in Santa Fe soon followed. A lawsuit (Anaya vs. PNM) brought forth on behalf of Santa Fe acequia associations was settled in 1992, and mandated a significant shift in water distribution philosophy. The judgment forced the water company to generate downstream releases for the purpose of irrigation for the first time in over a century, and put limits on the amount of water the dams could impound each year.

By 1978, Two-Mile Dam had deteriorated and was deemed a hazard. The reservoir was drained in 1992 and breached two years later. The land surrounding the reservoir was donated by the water company to The Nature Conservancy, and is now a nature preserve. Water still collects in what was once the reservoir bottom, creating wildlife habitat and groundwater recharge. The trail winding through the preserve gives visitors a tour of one of the greenest spaces in the Santa Fe watershed that is open to the public.

In the last few years, efforts have begun to mend some of the more significant damage to the river. USDA Forest Service watershed restoration efforts thinned trees in the upper watershed to reduce wildfire threat. This multi-year timber stand improvement has hand-thinned about 3,000 acres to alleviate overcrowding and to reduce the density of trees per acre from 800-1000 to a more natural 100-200. After several years, scientists will be able to evaluate whether thinning increases the amount of water entering the river via runoff.

Channel restoration efforts are underway below downtown Santa Fe. At San Ysidro crossing near Agua Fria, the County of Santa Fe has acquired conservation easements along the channel. The necessary construction work is underway to: (1) redistribute sediment from the steep, raw banks to the channel bottom, (2) raise the bed, (3) plant streamside vegetation, and (4) allow the river to interact with its floodplain. With the necessary money and support, their efforts are intended to continue downstream.

Also important to river restoration is the presence of water. As it stands today, the river flows only after the dams and acequias receive their share, and as a result, the presence of water is seasonal, and rare. There are no water rights for the river. The idea of a living river includes having a continuous flow, albeit very small. This year-round flow would recharge groundwater, supply native streamside vegetation, create a migratory route, and habitat for amphibians, fish, and songbirds within the corridor. Benefits to river water are not just environmental. Visitors and residents of Santa Fe flock to the river when it is wet, and partake in recreational opportunities like bird watching, fishing, and in the heaviest flows, kayaking. Utility bills now give residents the option to donate money towards purchasing a water right for the river. The city matches each private contribution, and will be responsible for purchasing the water right.

The story of the Santa Fe River is complex: climate, geology, and human factors all contribute to explain the current state of river hydrology and geomorphology. Throughout its use and abuse, the river remains a keystone in

Santa Fe history. Now, steps are being taken to reverse some of the effects of dams, while still benefiting from them. As science moves forward within the watershed, and more is understood about the physical system, humans will be able to better mimic nature in the river while meeting the future challenges posed by needs of the growing community and the unknowns of global climate change.

Acknowledgements:
The author would like to thank the following authors and contributors: Cordelia Snow, David Snow, Connie Woodhouse, Z. Spiegel and B. Baldwin, Malcolm Ebright, Sandy Hurlocker, Phil Bové, and Karen Lewis, and thank you KCR, for always encouraging me regardless of the mode.

Sources:
Spiegel, Z. and Baldwin, B. 1963. *Geology and Water Resources of the Santa Fe Area, New Mexico.* UGS Water Supply Paper 1525. Washington, D.C.: Government Printing Office.

Dr. Tara Plewa received her PhD in Geography from the University of South Carolina. She specializes in fluvial geomorphology, Geographic Information Systems (GIS), watershed science, and water policy and law. Her dissertation explored the natural and cultural history of the Santa Fe River over the last four centuries, and the environmental impact of humans within the watershed.

My Playground Was a River

Eliza Kretzmann

My connection to the Santa Fe River begins with a sky so blue it hurts the eyes, hills spotted with juniper and cactus, and green splashes of cottonwood along an intermittent stream. It begins with my birth in a land of contradictions, a high arid landscape stretched beneath a sweep of rustling aspen in the mountains above. Through this landscape cuts the lifeblood of Santa Fe—its River—the reason for Santa Fe's existence, and a potent part of my own personal history.

My earliest memories are interwoven with the river. I walked its banks, scaled its trees, collected smooth, shiny river rocks, and built mud castles along its shore. I remember expanses of lush grassy banks, the magic of river insects and wildlife. On summer evenings I'd squint at the river from my porch through the clothes hanging on the line, looking fearfully for *La Llorona*, the ghost of a woman rumored to roam the riverbanks. The river always seemed to be rich, alive, mystical. I loved and feared it.

When I was six, I played often in the river and its tributaries with my childhood friend, Ariela. We traced footprints in sand, collected twisted branches and leaves, and created mischievous and magical stories about the place. One spring day we heard a roar in the distance. We clambered out of the arroyo and in our rush, Ariela left a single red shoe on the arroyo floor. A wall of water crashed through the channel below us, and Ariela's shoe was swept away.

I played in the river with my sister almost every day in the summers. I was small, my sister gangly and tall. She easily scampered up a cottonwood that sloped over the water, her laughing face peering down at me. I was afraid to climb the tree. She tied a long, strong rope, and we swung out over the water. When the river swelled enough, we leapt into the shallow stream, creating a splash. We considered this our special kingdom. The river cultivated our sense of wilderness, creativity and curiosity. It also cultivated a bit of sibling rivalry. In fact, the English word "rival" comes from the Latin word "*rivalis*," meaning "someone sharing a river." My sister and I competed to see who could climb the tallest trees, who took the bravest swings, and who would be crowned River Queen for a season.

Even at a young age I wandered the river alone. I explored the nooks and crannies of my constant yet changing friend, the river. In the sandy rocks I sought treasure, like someone combing a beach after a storm. The best thing I ever found was a tin tea box with the Mandarin Orange lady on the lid. She became the goddess of the river to me, beautiful and otherworldly. I carried my treasures in this box for years.

The river itself contained treasure. I remember walking along the bank across from my house with my dad. The trees above were green, swaying in the wind. "Look," he said, pointing to a willow. It was covered, simply covered, with bold orange and black monarch butterflies.

Today the river has changed its face once again. In the spring it still has furious, raging flows. Sometimes these are even fiercer than those of my childhood, as more development and pavement yields more rushing waters. Frequently, however, the flow is sluggish or completely nonexistent. Walking over the downtown bridge over the water I often see an insipid flow, and usually it is a strange, stagnant color. Gone are the masses of monarch butterflies. Today the Santa Fe River is designated the "most endangered" river in the United States. This river, the very river that the city of Santa Fe and my own personal history is built upon, is dwindling. Jerome Delli Priscoli, senior policy analyst at the Institute of Water Resources, writes: "Water is one of our enduring human symbols of life, regeneration, purity and hope. It is one of our potent links with the sacred, with nature and with our cultural inheritance." I can only hope that the Santa Fe River, our own symbol of regeneration and life, will recover and thrive. Our very cultural and environmental identity, as well as our wildlife and water sources, may depend on it.

Eliza Kretzmann is the Executive Director of the Railyard Stewards. She formerly served as the Community Stewardship Coordinator at Earth Works Institute, and as an Associate at River Source, a small environmental consulting business. She has a BA in Environmental Studies from Pitzer College, and a Master of Public Administration degree in Environmental Science and Policy from Columbia University's School for International and Public Affairs.

Ode to the Santa Fe River

Andrew Leo Lovato

Humble and ever-present
You wind your way down Alameda Street like a magnet
Attracting the souls of those seeking refuge
An excuse for contemplation on a busy day

I grow old with you my friend
You are the ears of my innermost whisperings
When no one understood
Or lent the time to listen

Many afternoons I sat on your grassy shoulders
Looking down into the trickling stream of your life-blood
Searching for meaning in the ancient communion of man and water
A meditation with no peer, a mantra of the highest vibration

I peered over your side as a child
My fishing pole in hand
Waiting for a rainbow trout to choose my bait
From among a multitude of hopeful casters

I sang to you in my youth, strumming my guitar
Composing songs fed by idealism and sincerity
You did not laugh at my virgin attempts at expression
Instead you respectfully absorbed my prayers into your massive heart

I sat on your banks discussing the meaning of life
With sages and homeless vagabonds (often one in the same) on timeless summer
    days.
How can I ever forget Juanito's indescribable description
Concerning the delicacy of rattlesnake meat when cooked over a campfire?

I brought countless books from the Santa Fe Library
Returning to you, my most opulent easy chair
I fell in love with my future wife sitting near you as we shared our hearts
Speaking words of love to the accompaniment of your gentle voice

My children stepped into your cold, clean mountain water
Giggling in joy as you went on your way
I still visit you when life becomes too complicated
When I need to still my mind and draw from your simple wisdom

I am not your only lover
You gave generously to countless admirers before me
You who witnessed so much as history washed before you
Never did you refuse to give of your comfort despite the benefactor

Do you recall the Ancient Ones who built their villages near you in the early days?
The noble Spaniards on their horses who named the ground around you Santa Fe?
Did you take notice when you became a part of the United States in 1912?
Now you feel the weight of the growing tide of people surrounding you

Yet you remain stoic and loyal, even as we push you beyond your endurance
It is now time to give back to you, my amigo
There are those who see your plight and feel for you like a beloved father
Bear your load a little longer; relief is on its way

Claro que sí; como debe de ser

Andrew Leo Lovato is the author of *Santa Fe Hispanic Culture: Preserving Identity in a Tourist Town*. He has a PhD in Communication, and is an assistant professor at the Santa Fe Community College's School of Liberal Arts and Core Studies.

Santa Fe River in flood, collapsed bridge in distance. Date unknown. Sylvia Loomis
Photograph Collection. Courtesy New Mexico State Records Center and Archives. Image No.
21989.

Residents Oppose Paving of Riverbed
Maria Higuera
Journal North
May 5, 1983

During the 1980s, stories about the paving of the Santa Fe Riverbed filled the news. The plan, which focused on a downtown "River Park," was seriously considered until being firmly derailed by community opposition.

With few exceptions, Santa Fe residents opposed Wednesday an Army Corps of Engineers flood control plan that includes paving about a mile of the Santa Fe River bed between Delgado and Defouri streets.

The proposed $6.2 million project would also fund the reconstruction of six downtown bridges, a part of the plan that was as praised as the paving was attacked.

Lt. Col. Julian Pylant said, however, that the channel work and new bridges would have to be built together: "We're down to a project as we've described it or a no-action alternative."

Acting under congressional mandate, the corps is trying to provide protection from the 100-year flood, a theoretical calculation of peak flood conditions likely to occur within a 100-year period.

Plans to build low retaining walls outside the river bed were also attacked. But Peter Doles, project manager for the corps, said the walls weren't necessary anyway.

Pylant said that the corps, which first became involved in Santa Fe's flood problem in 1957, wants a response on its latest plan from the City Council within two months. "Your City Council is going to have to give us an indication whether they want us to go ahead," he told a crowd of about 80 people who attended the public hearing at City Hall. City Councilor Richard Catanach, an engineer, was the only elected official present.

The city would have to pay for 35%, or about $2.2 million of the project. Upon completion, the city would also become liable for the project and responsible for its maintenance.

State Engineer Steve Reynolds questioned the efficiency of

lining one mile of a 25 mile river. He also said that the best protection would be to store water upstream, east of Nichols Reservoir. "The floods in '57 and '68 came in below those reservoirs," he said.

A federal law of 1976, however, would have to be changed to allow construction of a third dam, above the existing ones.

Jay Lazarus, county hydrologist, said that paving would obstruct the recharge of the aquifer below the river. He also claimed that it would aggravate erosion further downstream by allowing the water to move more rapidly.

Several residents claimed that lining the river bed with concrete would destroy the aesthetics of the river park. The corps' proposal to paint the concrete brown and to "texture" it weren't sufficient.

Said D.D. Vansoelen, a lifelong resident, "I appreciate and love the aesthetics of the river bed. I walk along it every day on my way to work."

Vansoelen expressed the opinion of several speakers when he called the proposal, "an attempt at over-insurance."

James F. Kirkpatrick, owner and manager of the Inn at Loretto, said he doesn't want to risk lives at any cost. "I urge the adoption and timely construction of the corps' plan," he said.

Further, he said he would contribute $50,000 of the city's share of the project if construction were begun within the next two years.

Bridge crossing at Galisteo Street. Courtesy Palace of the Governors Photo Archive (NMHM/DCA). Negative No. 15328.

Santa Fe River Review

George Johnson

Shutting Down the River Again
June 2, 2005

The return of the Santa Fe River this spring has not only staved off the death of more willows and cottonwoods. It has helped to revive a city whose primary natural resource—its charm—is constantly threatened with extinction from overdevelopment.

The reason for the reprieve, of course, has been an unusually wet winter and spring, creating more mountain runoff than the city can hold behind its two upstream dams. But there is no reason why, with careful planning, there cannot be a threshold of water running through Santa Fe all the time. The sound and the sight of a living river do not have to be a meteorological fluke. Nor does it have to be something determined by unelected city water officials.

Today's newspaper reports that with the runoff now diminishing, the Water Division plans to cut off the flow entirely within the next two weeks. Barring a freak early summer thunderstorm, the river will be bone dry until at least late July when the monsoons begin. Then, if the dams become brim full again, the water bureaucrats will lend us our river back.

More than the drought, this feast and famine approach is what is damaging the riparian corridor. Had it the will, the City Council and Mayor could decide to adopt a policy of evening out the flow. Instead of no water for months on end punctuated by an erosional surge, we could have a real river— well, sometimes just a creek—continually running through the center of town. This would be good for trees, good for the community, and (like it or not) even good for tourism.

Taking Back the River
August 21, 2006

Early last summer after a bounteous snow melt filled the reservoirs and water poured down the Santa Fe River, bringing kayakers and trout fishermen to the middle of town, the Water Division was asked to study the feasibility of guaranteeing a minimal flow throughout the summer and fall. Impossible, the water czars concluded. Maintaining a running river would require an acre-foot per mile per day, or two cubic feet per second. Reaching as far west as, say, St. Francis Drive would mean releasing 484 acre-feet over a four-month period — 12 percent of the reservoirs' capacity, enough to provide precisely 3,227 people with drinking water. Everyone, including the council and the newspapers, let the matter drop. The Water Division's analysis was little more than an exercise in spreadsheet propaganda. Of course 3,227 people would not be denied hydration. The wells might have to be pumped a little harder until the Rio Grande Diversion came on line — regrettable but not nearly so bad as letting hundred-year-old cottonwoods die or risking a bosque fire in a canyon with just one way out. Even more disingenuous was the notion that the 484 acre-feet amounted to "lost water." Some of it, depending on the porosity of the soil, would seep into the ground recharging the very aquifer tapped by the city well field. We would be taking the same water through a different straw.

Finally, the report overlooked the fact that as water flowed out of the reservoirs, more would be flowing in. Whenever McClure and Nichols fill to the brim, the surplus must be discharged — in one erosional swoosh. Some of the modest portion of water allowed to bypass the dams would be water that would have to be released anyway.

But that wasn't what the Delgado Administration and its allies wanted to hear. One City Councilor said he could see no "tangible sense" in using publicly owned water for "aesthetic" purposes. (The river doesn't flow through his district.) Instead we were offered once again a pie-in-the-sky plan to pump effluent 12 miles and a thousand feet uphill from the sewage treatment plant on Airport Road to the top of Canyon Road and let it run back down.

No one seriously believes that will happen, and not just because of soaring energy and construction costs. Treated effluent has become a commodity. The city uses it to irrigate parks and other public land. It sells it to Las Campañas for its golf course and to construction companies for controlling dust and mixing concrete. There is only so much to go around. The cheaper, more efficient way to give water back to the river would be to let a small amount flow past the reservoirs all of the time.

During this Venusian summer, as much as 30 to 46 acre feet a day have been funneling in from the watershed. Letting go of just a fraction of that — 4 acre-feet — is all it would take to restore a shallow flow through downtown. Double the amount and the water might reach Frenchy's Field.

Even in drier times — especially in drier times — the city's water budget should include a line item for the river: of the inflow measured at the McClure gauge, a specified percentage would be released downstream. The reservoirs, now at 83 percent and rising, would fill a little more slowly, but what a small price to pay for having our river back again.

Flash flood on West Alameda, 1966. Albert Photograph Collection. Courtesy New Mexico State Records Center and Archives. Image No. 25556.

Santa Fe's Dying River Plan
January 28, 2007

Hard as it is to imagine, in a couple of months the mountain snowpack will start melting, overflowing the reservoirs, already 83% full, and flushing out the river from Nichols Reservoir to the Rio Grande. A few weeks later the runoff will slacken and the city will shut down the river again. Through the driest, hottest part of the year not a drop will be released from the dams. The cottonwoods and other vegetation will wither, the threat of a bosque fire will increase, and the city will continue approving new subdivisions.

Except for the very worst of the drought years, more water flows from the mountains and into the upper Canyon dams than the city has the legal right to use. In an average year the excess is around 1,500 acre-feet. The water is going to be released into the lower river anyway. With better planning it could be done gradually instead of in one fell swoop. There would be a small perennial flow from spring through autumn, more recharge of the aquifer, and the city would still get the 5,040 acre-feet it claims.

Judging from the news coverage and a conversation I had over dinner last fall with two of the Mayor's confidantes, nothing like that is even on the table. The so-called Living River plan is as vague, un-ambitious, and distant as ever.

"I look forward to a day when children don't ask where the Santa Fe River is because they can see the living river and tell us about it," Mr. Coss declared last year in his state of the city address. If he can only muster the political courage, that day could be now.

~rcr~

For years, award winning science writer George Johnson has kept tabs on Santa Fe's City Hall and beyond on his blog, The Santa Fe Review (http://santafereview.com). His "Dispatches from the Land and Water Wars" have kept a careful and sometimes critical eye on policy makers and developers that have neglected the Santa Fe River. These excerpts are drawn from three years of observation. Johnson's most recent book is The Ten Most Beautiful Experiments.

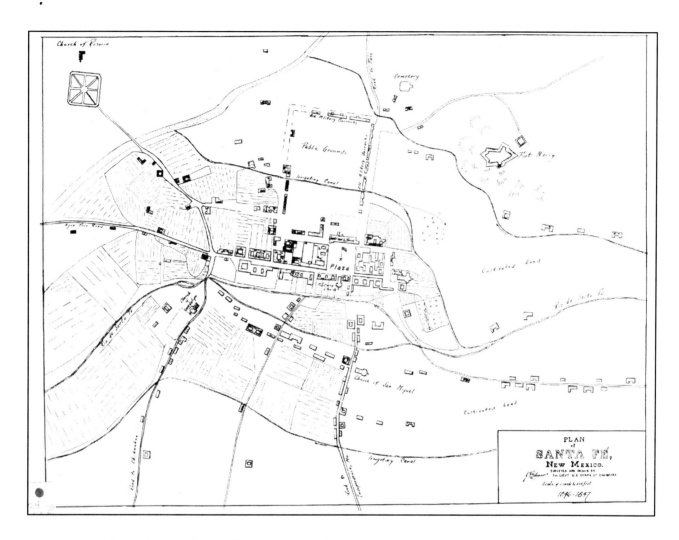

Plan of Santa Fe by JF Gilmer, 1846-1847. Courtesy Palace of the Governors, Fray Angélico Chávez History Library. Call# 78.9C S231.

Part of the Whole

Susan Tixier

Heraclites may have said, "On those stepping into rivers the same, other, and other river flow. We both step and do not step in the same river. We are and are not." Time, motion, and place, all together in a channel that doesn't change or move so much. But the river does move. And it changes. The philosophic questions of life are to be discovered at…a river. We become a part of a whole at…a river.

Sitting in the shade to meditate, walking barefoot in the summer, and stomping down the winter snowbanks along our Santa Fe River, always the same river, I and it together flowed through my life and the lives of my children. My son was blessed by it, in utero, when I slipped on the ice and fell into "the falls" in the Santa Fe River east of Delgado four or five months into my first pregnancy. My daughter learned and expressed an important lesson when she saw and objected in tears to a policeman dragging a homeless person from the river, beating him with a nightstick. "It's not fair," she said; a lesson learned for life. When my granddaughter, mother to my great granddaughter, was left at age three in my care, she and I walked the river, west of Guadalupe Street, exploring the wildlife, vegetation as if it were a truly wild river. To her, it was. And it is to each person who visits it, young or old, and sees its wildness.

Not just my story, but that of the Southwest can be found in the same river that exists here today. My children's ancestor came to what would be New Mexico from France, with Bishop Lamy. La Posada de Santa Fe, where I had my wedding reception 47 years ago, where I have been tending bar, was founded by Mr. Staab, a German Jew who settled in Santa Fe. Travelers gathered at that site years before pavement, next to the river. Santa Fe was the first national capital that America conquered in our Manifest Destiny; Americans watered their thirsty horses at the river. The little Santa Fe River, the same river, has been there through that time. And before.

The Santa Fe River has quenched thirsts, watered crops, provided shade and respite. It was and is in my life, one of the veins in my hands. It bears the history of the place and of the people of that place, the same river. And not the same river.

We know now that all things are connected. We see the river. We walk along the Alameda and we become part of the whole. We know it whether we "know" it or not.

If it is allowed to disappear, the place and the people will continue. History will be written and celebrated. We will go on. But the whole will have been destroyed. Someone once said that we ought to keep all the parts as we consider how best to be in the world. Someone else said that we ought to keep the instructions. The river is the instructions. It "tells" us how to be.

Lawyer, philosopher, bartender, and occasional farmer, librarian, and substitute teacher, Susan Tixier is a former director of Forest Guardians and Great Old Broads for Wilderness. She holds Master's degrees in Liberal Arts and Eastern Classics from St. John's College.

El Río

Fernando Garavito

En memoria de Priscilla Welton

Cualquier día el río salió de las manos de Dios.
Antes no existían las llanuras ni las montañas,
y no había riberas ni vertientes,
ni pequeños valles para que las aguas descansaran de su agitado ir
     y venir,
ni precipicios para que cayeran en un abismo sin fondo.
Entonces el río comenzó a ir a ciegas
y a tropezar una vez y mil veces,
a enredarse en sus propias aguas y corrientes
y a avanzar por un camino sin retorno.
Era la época en que las cosas apenas comenzaban
y había terremotos y volcanes
y los continentes navegaban por las aguas del mar
como barcos abiertos con todas las velas desplegadas.
En medio de ese cataclismo
el río llegó a todas las regiones, se cobijó bajo todos los cielos,
fue él mismo bajo las aguas del mar
y él mismo al subir a las cumbres nevadas
a tratar de ser eterno bajo la mirada del sol.
Fue entonces cuando nacieron los hombres
que aprendieron a ir hasta sus orillas
a cumplir oficios tan sencillos como descansar o jugar a la pelota,
o inventarse lenguajes para poder hablar.
Junto a él crecieron palabras transparentes como la palabra agua,
o términos para soñar, como la palabra vuelo y la palabra camino,
y también la palabra muerte que es el vuelo que no termina jamás.
Poco a poco los hombres aprendieron a entrar en el río, a atravesarlo,
algunos se aventuraron a ir un poco más allá de la primera curva,
muchos se hirieron con las piedras del fondo
o hundieron los pies en las arenas o sintieron entre las piernas
la caricia estremecedora de las anguilas
o se dejaron llevar por la corriente hasta los remolinos,

The River

Fernando Garavito
English Translation by Theo Walker

In memory of Priscilla Welton

On a day like any other the river left the hands of God.
Before, there were no plains or mountains,
no riverbanks, no mountain slopes,
nor tiny valleys where the waters might rest from their turbulent comings
    and goings,
nor cliffs where they might fall into an endless chasm.
So the river began to advance blindly
and stumble once and a thousand times,
to tangle itself up in its waters and currents,
and to go forward on a path of no return.
It was the epoch when things were just beginning
and there were earthquakes and volcanoes
and the continents navigated the ocean waters
like ships adrift with their sails unfurled.
In the midst of this cataclysm
the river appeared in every region, took shelter beneath every sky,
was the very same beneath the waters of the sea
as it was in its ascent of the snowy mountain-peaks
in an attempt to become eternal beneath the gaze of the sun.
It was then that men were born
who would learn to make their way as far as the banks of the river
busying themselves with occupations as simple as relaxing or playing ball,
or inventing languages so they might speak.
By the river grew translucent words like the word water,
or terms for dreaming, like the word flight and the word road,
and also the word death which is the flight that never ends.
Little by little men learned to enter the river, to cross it,
a few ventured a little further beyond the first curve,
many hurt themselves on the rocks at the bottom
or sank their feet into the sands or felt between their legs
the shuddering caress of eels
or let themselves be carried away by the currents as far as the whirlpools,

donde terminaron por ahogarse
asombrados ante la fuerza misteriosa del conocer y el conocerse.
Así, el río fue la sed y fue el agua para saciarla,
fue el viaje y el hecho de embarcarse,
y la nave y el viento para correr entre las velas.
Cierta vez uno de ellos quiso ir hasta el límite.
Iba con la mirada que tienen los iluminados,
el cayado y la brújula y un zurrón para llevar los alimentos
y una honda para cazar y para defenderse del peligro.
"Ya volveré," les dijo a los demás, "cuando sepa qué existe más allá del allá,
cuando vea con mis propios ojos qué esconden los meandros,
y compruebe cómo las lianas dejan caer su línea dorada desde las copas de los
        árboles,
para que en ellas las mariposas encuentren la forma de ser aéreas en su universo
        de colores."
Entonces comenzó a pasar el tiempo hasta que todos lo olvidaron.
De vez en cuando alguien tenía sobre él una memoria trémula,
que no lograba precisar ni el por qué ni el para qué de un viaje,
que en el oficio de los términos alguien llamó odisea,
palabra que, tal vez, quiera decir viaje en el laberinto.
Pasaron trescientos años, quizás uno más, uno menos,
hasta que cierto día un hombre quiso entrar a una casa que no era su casa.
En la mirada tenía la visión de las aguas profundas,
y su barba estaba poblada de ramas secas y de arbustos,
las orejas le habían crecido para oír los sonidos del mundo,
y sus palabras decían cosas olvidadas por todos,
como catalejo o astrolabio o rosa de los vientos.
"Soy el que fui," dijo el hombre ante los ojos asombrados
de quienes recordaban haber oído hablar de él, como una leyenda,
que venía desde el tiempo de los abuelos de los abuelos de sus padres.
"No alcancé a llegar hasta el fin del mundo que es el sitio donde termina el río,
pero en él conocí el fuego misterioso que abriga el corazón de la mujer,
y fue en ese corazón donde me sumergí en un misterio infinito;
estuve, también, con los cíclopes y con los unicornios;
en la tribu de los reducidores de cabezas
me senté al pie del estrado donde escriben los autores de dogmas y de doctrinas,
y allí comprobé que sus palabras provocan cambios en el curso del río,
que se ve obligado a buscar senderos donde el aire no esté contaminado,
y vertientes donde no haya espejismos."
"He acumulado en mí—dijo el hombre—el conocimiento del mundo.
Debo escribirlo para que quienes vengan después no pierdan esa memoria.
Tal vez me demore doscientos años o más en terminarla,
pero en ella estará todo lo que es necesario saber,

where they ended up drowning
astonished before the mysterious power of knowing and knowing oneself.
Thus, the river became thirst and the water to satisfy it,
it was the trip and the embarking,
and the boat and the wind to ripple through the sails.
Once, one of them decided to go to the limit.
He left with the look that illuminati have,
with a staff and compass and a pouch for food,
and a sling to hunt and defend himself from danger.
"I will return," he told the others, "when I know what exists beyond the beyond,
when I see with my own eyes what the twistings and turnings conceal,
and discover how the lianas let their golden line fall from the tree-tops,
so that butterflies may discover the way to be aerial in their universe of colors."
Then time began to pass until everyone forgot him.
Now and then someone had a tremulous memory of him,
    and could not be sure of the why or wherefore of a journey,
which in the realm of terms someone called odyssey,
a word that, perhaps, may mean a journey in the labyrinth.
Three hundred years passed, maybe one more, one less,
until one day a man tried to enter a house which was not his house.
In his gaze he had the vision of deep waters,
and his beard was full of dry branches and shrubs,
his ears had grown so as to hear the sounds of the world,
and his words said things forgotten by all,
such as spyglass or astrolabe or gyrocompass.
"I am the one who left," spoke the man before the astonished eyes
of those who remembered having heard of him, like a legend,
which went back to the time of the grandfathers of the grandfathers of their
        fathers.
"I did not reach the end of the world, the place where the river ends,
but in it I did discover the mysterious fire that warms the heart of woman,
and it was in that heart that I immersed myself in infinite mystery;
I was also with the Cyclops and the Unicorns;
in the tribe of the head-shrinkers
I sat at the foot of the platform where the authors of dogmas and doctrines write,
and there I realized that their words change the course of the river,
which must then search for paths where the air is not contaminated,
where the slopes are free of mirages."
"I hold within myself," spoke the man, "the knowledge of the world.
I must write it down so that those who come after do not lose this memory.
It may take two hundred years or more to finish,
but it will contain everything that needs to be known,

desde la existencia de Dios, al que llamaré con todos los nombres conocidos,
hasta los elementos, y las leyes de la física y de la botánica.
Comprobaré que la Tierra es plana y que está en el centro de la creación,
que el hombre es a su vez el centro de ese centro, y que su conciencia
es la que impulsa lo creado y lo que aún está por crearse;
describiré los animales, las categorías de los ángeles, los círculos del infierno;
precisaré las leyes naturales y me extenderé sobre el trivium y el quadrivium,
diré qué es verdad y, al hacerlo, le pondré fin a los cismas y a los sofismas,
cualquiera tendrá sobre su mesa el río que recorrí palmo a palmo,
al abrir sus páginas encontrará las selvas y las estrellas
y oirá los vientos huracanados y las tempestades que se levantan en el centro del
    mar."
El hombre selló sus labios y se dedicó a su tarea.
En un comienzo todos veían la lucecita de su habitación encendida hasta la
    madrugada,
pero poco a poco fueron olvidándolo mientras cada cual se dedicaba a sus asuntos,
los campesinos a sembrar el trigo y a cosechar el milagro del pan en la cocina,
los herreros a forjar las coronas del rey y las herraduras de las bestias,
la muerte a distribuir las epidemias y a ahondar en el dolor y la miseria.
Mucho tiempo después (como esta es una historia antigua
ya nadie recuerda las fechas ni las anécdotas),
un muchacho quiso atravesar el pueblo acortando camino por las habitaciones.
Al abrir esa puerta que nadie tocaba desde años inmemoriales,
una bocanada de aire fresco lo golpeó de lleno en el rostro y el pecho.
Allí estaba el hombre, recostado sobre su mesa,
y en el libro que tenía abierto ante sí se alcanzaba a leer la palabra "umbral"
escrita con caligrafía minuciosa. El muchacho llamó a los vecinos:
"vengan," "vengan," gritó a voz en cuello mientras del libro
salían las guacamayas de colores que sólo se conocen en los mares del sur,
salían Islandia y el Taj Mahal y la Tierra del Fuego,
y un conejo vestido de etiqueta consultando su reloj de bolsillo,
aparte de un globo aerostático y Louis Pasteur junto a su microscopio,
y la Muralla China aplastada por la solemnidad de los emperadores,
y el Réquiem escrito para sí mismo por un hombre joven que murió de fiebres
    reumáticas,
y la ballena blanca perseguida por un marino hundido en la demencia…
Después, cuando volvió la calma,
cuando cada una de las cosas hubo tomado su rumbo cierto y distinto
hacia el sitio que llegarían a ocupar en la memoria de los hombres,
surgió del libro una última figura. Era leve
y venía envuelta en la armonía de sus movimientos,
que salían de su fuerza interior, de su serena mirada profunda.

from the existence of God, whom I will call by all the known names,
to the elements, as well as the laws of physics and botany.
I will prove that the Earth is flat and that it is at the center of creation,
that man is in turn the center of that center, and that his consciousness
is that which drives the created and what is yet to be created;
I will describe the animals, the categories of angels, the circles of hell;
I will precisely state the natural laws and expound the trivium and quadrivium,
I will say what is the truth, and by doing so, I will put an end to schisms and
    sophisms,
anyone may have upon their table the river I explored step by step,
when they open its pages they will discover jungles and stars,
and they will hear the winds of the hurricanes and the tempests that surge at the
    center of the sea."
The man sealed his lips and devoted himself to his labor.
At the beginning everyone saw the lamp of his dwelling lit until dawn,
but little by little they began to forget him as they went about their business,
the field-workers to sow the wheat and harvest the miracle of bread in the kitchen,
the iron-workers to forge the crowns of the king and the horseshoes of the beasts,
death to distribute epidemics and deepen its command of pain and misery.
Much later (since this is an ancient story
no one now remembers the dates or the details),
a boy thought to take a shortcut through the village by going through the
    dwellings.
When he opened the door that no one had knocked at since time immemorial,
a breath of fresh air hit him square in the face and chest.
There was the man, reclining on the table,
and in the book before him a word could be made out, "threshold,"
written in a meticulous script. The boy called the neighbors:
"come," "come," he shouted while from the book
emerged macaws in colors only seen in the South Seas,
Iceland appeared and the Taj Mahal and Tierra del Fuego,
and a rabbit in evening dress consulting his pocket-watch,
as well as a hot-air balloon and Louis Pasteur beside his microscope,
and the Great Wall of China squashed by the solemnity of the emperors,
and the Requiem written for and by a young man who died of rheumatic fever,
and a white whale pursued by a sailor drowning in madness...
Later, when calm was restored,
when each thing had taken its true and distinct course
toward the place that it would occupy in the memory of men and women,
one last figure emerged from the book. She was light
and drew near enveloped in the harmony of her movements,
which came from her power within, from her serene and profound gaze.

Ella era la brisa que detiene el curso de las tempestades,
la encrucijada que señala el mejor de los caminos posibles,
en sus brazos nacían los vientos alisios,
y su sonrisa era un rayo de sol sobre un magnolio cubierto de rocío.
"El conocimiento es infinito," dijo con una voz tranquila,
que se oyó como el agua que fluye en los arroyos de los campos.
"Cada uno de nosotros lo seguirá como se sigue la corriente de un río que se
    bifurca.
Todos bajarán hasta su orilla, pero no todos se hundirán en sus aguas,
algunos lo remontarán con dificultad, pero los más irán corriente abajo,
sin que ninguno encuentre jamás su nacimiento o su desembocadura,
algunos avanzarán más que otros, algunos se sentarán en una piedra a contemplar
    el infinito,
otros sufrirán la desazón de quien sabe qué debe hacer pero no sabe cómo hacerlo.
Pasarán muchos siglos pero algún día llegará el tiempo
en que el hombre encontrará la mejor manera de enfrentar sus desafíos,
y habrá algunos que sabrán cómo ayudar a los demás a seguir su camino…"
Cuando su figura comenzó a esfumarse en el aire,
aquel que la amó por el sólo hecho de verla, quiso saber quién era,
y ella, con una voz que se perdió en el tiempo, alcanzó a contestarle:
"Me llamo Priscilla Welton. Fui maestra."

~~~

Fernando Garavito nació en Bogotá, Colombia, en 1944. Su infancia transcurrió en un poblado extendido a orillas de un riachuelo sin nombre, tal vez el "río de la aldea" de Pessoa, tan insignificante que junto a él solo pudo soñar en ríos infinitos. Ha publicado dos libros de poemas: *Já*, e *Ilusiones y Erreciones*, y una antología de su trabajo literario, *Banquete de Cronos*. Vivió en los Estados Unidos desde el año 2002, hasta que falleció repentinamente en 2010.

She was the breeze that halts the course of tempests,
the crossroads that shows the best of all possible paths,
in her arms the trade winds were born,
and her smile was a ray of sunlight upon the magnolia covered in dew.
"Knowledge is infinite," she said in a tranquil voice,
which sounded like the water that flows through the streams of the fields.
"Each one of us will follow it like the current of a river that forks.
All will go down to its banks, but not all will sink into its waters,
Some upstream will arduously make their way, but most will go downstream,
never finding its origin or where it ends,
some will go further than others, some will sit upon a rock to contemplate infinity,
others will suffer the grief of knowing what they ought to do but not knowing
    how to do it.
Many centuries will go by but one day the time will come
when people will discover the best way to face their challenges,
and there will be some who will know how to help others to follow their path..."
When the figure began to dissolve into the air,
one who loved her simply through having seen her, longed to know who it was,
and she, with a voice that was lost in time, could be heard to answer:
"My name is Priscilla Welton. I was a teacher."

~~~

Fernando Garavito was born in Bogotá, Colombia, in 1944. His childhood was passed in an extended village along the banks of a nameless stream, perhaps Pessoa's "river of the hamlet," so insignificant that before it he could only dream of infinite rivers like the one in this poem. He published two books of poems, *Ja*, and *Ilusiones y Erecciones*, as well as an anthology of his literary work, *Banquete de Cronos*. He lived in the United States from 2002 until passing away unexpectedly in 2010.

Theo Walker currently teaches Spanish in the Department of Spanish and Portuguese at UNM in Albuquerque. He is the translator of *Praxis and Ambiguity of the Enemy* by Fernando Garavito.

II

Sustenance and Loss

*Ay, del que junto al río
no quiere llamarse sed.*

Oh, Whoever stays by a river
won't ever know about thirst.

— Rosario Castellanos

The Unnamable River

Arthur Sze

1

Is it in the anthracite face of a coal miner,
crystallized in the veins and lungs of a steel
worker, pulverized in the grimy hands of a railroad engineer?
Is it in a child naming a star, coconuts washing
ashore, dormant in a volcano along the Rio Grande?

You can travel the four thousand miles of the Nile
to its source and never find it.
You can climb the five highest peaks of the Himalayas
and never recognize it.
You can gaze through the largest telescope
and never see it.

But it's in the capillaries of your lungs.
It's in the space as you slice open a lemon.
It's in a corpse burning on the Ganges,
in rain splashing on banana leaves.

Perhaps you have to know you are about to die
to hunger for it. Perhaps you have to go
alone into the jungle armed with a spear
to truly see it. Perhaps you have to
have pneumonia to sense its crush.

But it's also in the scissor hands of a clock.
It's in the precessing motion of a top
when a torque makes the axis of rotation describe a cone:
and the cone spinning on a point gathers
past, present, future.

2

In a crude theory of perception, the apple you
see is supposed to be a copy of the actual apple,
but who can step out of his body to compare the two?
Who can step out of his life and feel
the Milky Way flow out of his hands?

An unpicked apple dies on a branch;
that is all we know of it.
It turns black and hard, a corpse on the Ganges.
Then go ahead and map out three thousand miles of the Yangtze;
walk each inch, feel its surge and
flow as you feel the surge and flow in your own body.

And the spinning cone of a precessing top
is a form of existence that gathers and spins death and life into one.
It is in the duration of words, but beyond words—
river river river, river river.
The coal miner may not know he has it.
The steel worker may not know he has it.
The railroad engineer may not know he has it.
But it is there. It is in the smell
of an avocado blossom, and in the true passion of a kiss.

～～

Arthur Sze is the author of eight books of poetry, most recently *The Ginkgo Light*. He is the recipient of numerous awards, including a Lannan Literary Award for Poetry and an American Book Award. He is a professor emeritus at the Institute of American Indian Arts and was the first Poet Laureate of Santa Fe.

Rock, sand, and ripples on the Santa Fe River. Photograph by EC Ryan.

After Noon in Yootó

Luci Tapahonso

The Santa Fe afternoon is warm and bright.
The dogs are delirious to be outdoors; they prance about, panting loudly.
"Simmer down, guys," I say.
They don't have to wear jackets today.
Once my husband said they were embarrassed to wear jackets.
"I never saw a dog embarrassed," I said. He just smiled.

A few months ago on another warm afternoon,
my mother sat on the comfortable old couch in the front of the woodstove.
The stove is in the center of the house and the room is dim and cool.

After straightening the kitchen, I sat down beside her.
"Uh," I said leaning against her meaning "tell me stories,"
or "tell me what's going on."
"T'áá 'ákódí. That's all," she said. We both laughed.

I adjusted the pillow behind her head as she leaned back.
I slipped my hand into hers and leaned against her.
Her hands are warm and thin.
Unlike mine, she has slim, elegant fingers.
She patted my hand and we were silent.

We were alone in the quiet house.
Across the road, a cow bellowed and somewhere by the wash,
dogs were barking playfully. One sounded like a puppy.
Here in the living room, we rested and closed our eyes.
Then she said, with her eyes still closed, "Let's sing."
So I started a song and she joined in. I sang close to her so she could hear.
We sang several songs, then she started one and I was quiet.
"I don't know that one," I said after she opened her eyes and looked at me.
"You do," she said, "One time I heard you singing it."
She kept on singing and after a while, I got it and we finished.

"Whaa," she said, like she was tired.
She fell asleep. I kept holding her hand and leaning on her.
I wanted to sleep, but couldn't.
It seemed like there was too much going on,
but it was just she and I sitting together on a late summer afternoon.
Her cat, Kitty Baá, jumped on the couch and stretched out beside us.
It seemed that Kitty Bah and Mom always napped at the same time.

Today in Yootó, there's snow on the highest peaks
of the Sangre De Cristos — the mountain of the Blood of Christ.
The bright snow is startling against the deep blue sky.

It's warm enough to use the screen door;
The afternoon sun slants into the kitchen in thin lines.
The dogs sleep on the warm tile squares.

It's mid-October in Yootó where beads of clear, cold water
form an ancient necklace that encircle the Sangre de Cristos.

Luci Tapahonso is the author of three children's books and six books of poetry, including *A Radiant Curve: Poems and Stories*. A professor of English and American Indian Studies at the University of Arizona, Tapahonso is the recipient of many awards, including the 2009 Arizona Book Award for Poetry for *A Radiant Curve*. She divides her time between Tucson, Arizona, and Santa Fe, where her husband is president of the Institute of American Indian Arts.

A River Revived
Filled By Recent Rains and Melting Snow,
Reservoir Reaches Capacity and Overflows into Santa Fe River
Tom Sharpe
The Santa Fe New Mexican
April 15, 2004

Almost every spring at least some water runs into the river. On years when conditions are perfect – heavy snowpack combined with enough rain to keep municipal water use down – the river might flow for months. Other years, there might be considerable snowpack but dry conditions lead to an increased amount of water being drawn from the reservoirs. When this happens, the majority of incoming water is stored, and the river's season is cut short.

cce

It is a rare sight. The Santa Fe River – bone dry most of the time – started flowing Monday when Nichols Reservoir filled to capacity and began spilling over its dam up east of the city.

Recent rains and melting snowpack in the Santa Fe Canyon watershed have sent more than 9 million gallons a day into the city's two reservoirs.

McClure Reservoir, the larger and more upstream of the reservoirs, continues to rise by about a foot a day but has about 10 feet to go before it reaches its 862 million-gallon capacity.

Nichols Reservoir, however, reached its 223 million-gallon capacity early Monday and began dumping excess water into the riverbed, sending a steady stream through the heart of Santa Fe.

Mike Gonzales, city water-operations supervisor, said the overflow surprised him.

"I didn't even mention it at the (city Public Utilities Committee last week) because I wasn't sure what kind of moisture (the approaching storm) was going to bring," he said. "I thought, 'if it's snow, it won't really affect us that soon.' But it was rain, primarily rain, so the inflow started real quickly."

Gonzales estimated Wednesday that 7.5 million gallons a day are running down the Santa Fe River.

In addition to flow in the river, the Acequia Madre has been flowing off and on since last week when the ditch association opened its headgate near Cristo Rey Church.

Gonzales said the Acequia Madre was taking water from the flow of tributaries into the Santa Fe River downstream from the city reservoirs, not from releases from the reservoirs.

Together, the two reservoirs are filled to 85 percent of their combined capacity.

City Manager Jim Romero said the city will begin releasing more water when McClure Reservoir reaches 90 percent of capacity, partly to manage additional runoff.

Depending on weather over the next two months, the city could make controlled releases from its reservoirs until the end of June, peaking at as much as 30 million gallons a day, according to a city news release.

The city hasn't drawn from its reservoirs since last fall. The water treatment plant in Santa Fe canyon has been off-line for a major rehabilitation of its filter system so it can meet new federal drinking water standards. The plant is supposed to start operating again early next month.

The optimistic outlook for local spring runoff has the state Game and Fish Division looking to stock the Santa Fe River with rainbow trout for the first time in several years.

Rick Castell of the division's Northwest Area Operations Office in Albuquerque confirmed Wednesday that he has recommended stocking the Santa Fe River for a fishing derby on May 22, during the annual CommUNITY Days celebration.

Thirsty River

A. Kyce Bello

*E*very evening when the light turns golden and the Sangres glow red, my husband and I make our way to the Santa Fe River. The dry course we follow is a bed of sand and rock between high, eroded banks. We watch the clouds, pay attention as the trees drop and regain their leaves, notice the patterns left in the sand by wind and intermittent water. We come in all weathers and all moods, sharing the triumphs and challenges of our day or simply walking in silence. The river is our tonic, an open space curative that offers rejuvenation day after day. As the wheel of seasons turns, I grasp that this channel contains not water but the flow of our lives.

In the heart of winter Elliot and I are often the only people out at sunset, but as the weather warms and days lengthen, we begin to see our neighbors. Even on the finest days, however, we see no more than a handful of people, a few dogs sniffing the sand.

"Why aren't there more people here?" I ask Elliot one day. It seems strange that in a town full of nature lovers, this open space corridor is often abandoned.

"Maybe they don't realize this is the river," he says. "They forgot."

Once upon a time this river flowed like any other in northern New Mexico. It meandered down out of the mountains along a sandy bottomed, ground level bed surrounded by willows, cottonwoods, farms and meadows. As I walk the deep gash that is so easy to mistake for an impressive arroyo, I try to imagine what it once looked like. I can barely see it.

Gone are the native plants, the animals and fish that once thrived here. Denied water, the river's bed of sand has grown lifeless, its banks fallen in. The near horizon opens on barren fields. Fields where food was once grown, irrigated by arterial acequias. Those fields are called lots now, and everyone knows it won't be long until houses grow out of them.

After a half-mile or so of walking, the few cottonwoods and elm trees that grow along the path fade into grey-green chamisa and dried grasses. My friend Sarah won't walk this section of the river.

"It's too brown and dry," she says. "And so depressing." This is where the junk cars start to rise out of the brown earth, and the cholla grows thick as weeds. I have heard things like this before. Newcomers say, "I miss the ocean, trees, rain." They say, "You call this a river?"

I don't mean it to be, but my voice is sharp when I remind Sarah that the river is dry because we drink it.

Cholla cactus on high banks above the Santa Fe River. Photograph by EC Ryan.

One evening in March, Elliot and I abandon the river and walk up a ridge overlooking Santa Fe. The sun has just set, leaving a band of orange along the horizon.

"Where does the water for so many houses come from?" Elliot asks. "It should be sand running from these taps, not water."

I scan the dusk washed land. Junipers are sprinkled over a sea of dried grass. The piñons are gone, dead from the long drought we've been in. Lights shimmer in the black expanse stretching before us, blocks of light following the highway south. If there is enough water for all of these homes, how can there not be enough for the river?

Wherever the water comes from, too much is being asked of this land and too little is given back. The river that has supported settlements in this valley for over a thousand years no longer flows. It is a bed of sand. And the city grows, and grows, and grows.

As the days turn warm, the river begins to run with snowmelt. Muddy. Frothing. Roiling with the trash that has lain unwashed all winter. Foam swirls against concrete, against rock, against sandy riverbank.

Elliot and I squat side by side and watch the torrent. There's no crossing it tonight. The water splashes up against us, cold. If this river's singing, the song is a dirty one, the kind that pours from a downtown bar late on a Tuesday night. The river has reclaimed its channel, liberated by reinforcements of melted snow in the war against containment. It is like a prisoner whose face twists with anger, sadness, and relief when finally freed. A prisoner who runs away as quickly and violently as he can.

The water level changes slightly each day, leaving behind dark, wet spots in the muddy banks. Prints from people, dogs, and birds spatter across the damp sand. The metal caging that was supposed to protect the banks from erosion hangs empty. Tree roots caught in the wire mesh are all that remains of the soil they grew out of. Elsewhere, the path has literally fallen into the river. A new one runs through the cactus a bit farther from the river's center.

Decades ago, efforts to stabilize the banks led the Army Corps of Engineers to wrap heavy wire fencing against the river's sides. They strapped stones into retainer walls, and paved the riverbank with concrete rounded to look like rocks. The cutting of the riverbed was encouraged to safeguard the increasing density of downtown buildings from catastrophic floods.

This kind of "maintenance" reflects the way Santa Fe has perceived the river. It is an extension of our plumbing, a faucet that can literally be turned off and on at will. The river is the drain that carries wasted storm water away, but is not thought to need water of its own. When it starts running again, south of town, the water is treated effluent.

Up at the reservoirs, it is someone's job to decide how much water to release to the river, how much to hold. The city's water glass needs to be filled before the snow melts, but the reservoir must not overflow. It is a job that swings between stinginess and excess. I wonder how the person at the gate can bear to let any water loose, or to keep it contained.

In early April, the group American Rivers declares the Santa Fe the most endangered river in the country. It is strange news, coming at a time when the river has begun to run peacefully. The rush of water has slowed to an ankle deep ripple. It has found a curving path through the wide riverbed, and runs braided in the loveliest sections. The nondescript trees growing out of the rocky sand turn green. I am happy to see the color, but then realize the trees are Siberian elms, an invasive species. Other plants come up—mustards, mallows, verbena. Three cottonwoods burst open with the freshest, lightest green leaves imaginable. Finally, slender willow leaves emerge from the few pockets where they have survived.

Every afternoon, children can be heard playing in the water. Families go fishing. I see an elderly couple walking hand in hand, and later sitting and watching the water. A beaver has been sighted just east of the section Elliot and I walk each day after work. A beaver. We stay out past dusk in hopes of seeing it.

I have always taken pleasure in walking along the river, but now that it flows, just as its name suggests it should, a sense of wonder and gratitude overcomes me. It is the reverse of witnessing an amputation. Indeed, it is a resurrection.

Water flows again through the heart of our community, restoring a semblance of balance to the river. It is as if a special pair of glasses have been given to me, allowing me to glimpse the invisible thread that connects the willows and rocks, the wild alfalfa, the raven flying soundlessly overhead. Allowing me to see this oversized arroyo for what it is meant to be—a living, breathing, riparian ecology.

What else does the river offer that we have forgotten in our thirst for its liquid? Beyond mere sustenance, what else is carried in its arms?

While walking the river, I have awakened to its emptiness. Each time we take a drink, we drink the river. Instead of flowing along its course, it runs through our bodies. How can we not become attentive to the needs of the river, when it has been sacrificed to sustain us?

The empty riverbed is my responsibility because I, too, am a container for the river. In gratitude, it is time to return those waters to where they belong.

I am driving to work one morning before dawn on Alameda, parallel to the river. The sky behind the mountains is rich with pinks and reds. A great creature swoops in front of my car, flies low in front of me. It is a bird, I realize, slamming my brakes in surprise. A great blue heron flying upstream. My heart leaps into my throat. A heron on the Santa Fe River.

Migrations, rhythms, cycles. Before me is the hope of the river—a reminder of what has been broken and what will be healed. Before me is a fragment of balance.

At the hospital parking lot another nurse comes up to me. "I was driving behind you when the heron flew out," she says. Though we only know each other by sight, she takes my arm and squeezes it. "I wept when I saw that, and I was so glad someone else saw it too."

Our hearts are as broken as the river. It is time to piece this tapestry of ecology, of community, back together.

At an Earth Day celebration, the Santa Fe Watershed Association has a booth. They have two displays of river water habitats. A plastic basin holds river water from the Pecos River. Filled with floating leaves, dirt, and other natural debris, it is home to scores of bugs—stonefly, riffle beetle, dobsonfly, mayfly—and those only the ones visible to the naked eye. The signs of a robust, intact waterway.

Another plastic basin contains a sample from the Santa Fe River. It is dry, empty except for a few red rocks and some sand. Someone comes up behind me and asks if they can pour some water into the Santa Fe basin. After all, the river *is* running, even if it doesn't have any life to speak of. Most people agree that the beaver swam back to the Rio Grande.

I join the association. It seems like a small step, but never before have I translated my yearning for something, or my anger and frustration, into collective action. In her book, *The Open Space of Democracy*, Terry Tempest Williams challenges ecological complacency by asking, "At what point do we finally lay our bodies down to say this blatant disregard for biology and wild lives is no longer acceptable?" I have reached that point. I can no longer abide living a block from a river called most endangered in America. It is as if I have crossed a threshold and burst into passionate flames. Only a restored river can put this fire out.

It might be years before the Santa Fe River sees year round water and fully recovers from its degraded condition, but after a only a month or so of flow, it shows signs—like the heron and beaver, but smaller and perhaps more significant—of its return.

I marvel at the ability of the land to repair itself given a trickle of water and the attention of caring citizens. Dozens of small stone check-dams built by folks on their evening walks have done their work well, terracing the water flow and reshaping the riverbed. Sand bars have formed, and the river's bottom is now lined with rocks and pebbles. Most incredible of all is the algae. First a coat of slime on the river rocks, it grows into a thick moss, and finally begins streaming with the water. Yellow green growth where once lay dry red sand. The joy of water and light and plant cells.

It only makes my fire burn hotter.

The river might flow for months yet, until late June. Inevitably, it will stop. The river dries up, year after year. The willow and cottonwood stems planted in a burst of optimism—let's restore the living river!—will shrivel up and get washed away during a late summer monsoon.

"The world is going to be saved by people saving their own homes," Pete Seeger said. I am relieved to have found my way to this truth. The world's problems are too big for me. The river is a block from my house. I have known it in all weathers, all lights. I drink it in every glass of water from my sink. My heartbeat quickened when the heron swept across my path. Perhaps the world will be saved by people saving themselves.

I have heard people say, "There isn't enough water for the river. It would be wasted if it ran downstream. We need it for our homes, our businesses." The city hydrologist says that the river is considered a renewable resource, like wind power. What she means is that the water is renewable. It refills the reservoirs each spring after a wet winter, and thus can be used freely.

The river itself, however, is not renewable unless it is given water. The river is dying and will continue to die—its banks deepening and falling in, the native vegetation dead, the animals gone along with their habitat.

It is time for a reordering of priorities. A minimum amount of water necessary to sustain a living river should be released year round, period. If this were the case, we wouldn't go thirsty. We would adapt, learning very quickly to live within our means. Water conservation measures, including rain catchment and greywater systems, would become our way of providing for the future, as opposed to dependence on "foreign water" like the San Juan River.

The Santa Fe River is our physical connection to the past, a tangible link that connects the generations that have come before with those who will follow. It spans time and history, anchoring us to our home. It is the thread that stitches us back into the tapestry of the wild, pointing us gently away from destruction and towards conservation.

The river is the place where the natural world, the mythical world, the spiritual and the historical worlds enter our bodies, our minds. Without it, we are adrift. Our land becomes as meaningless as a textbook on the past, a story without life.

The feast day of San Isidro, patron saint of Agua Fria Village comes in late May. I slip into the back of the church and add my voice to the choir. The deacon leads us in praising San Isidro, thanking him for tending the fields, the orchards, the acequias, and the river.

A hand painted banner of the saint is carried down the church's aisle. Elderly women follow close behind the deacon; the choir with its guitars falls into step after them. The rest of us follow, singing the *alabado de San Isidro*. We proceed down the road, and turn towards the river. When the water comes into sight, there are dozens of people along its banks. Our voices grow stronger when we see them, and we carry the saint forward to those waters.

Flowers are handed out. Children give them to their grandmothers, to their neighbors, to conservationists and politicians. The deacon asks us to line up along the river, to raise our hands. He prays for the river, that it may flow and be strong, and that it bring spiritual strength to all in our community. We cry amen, *ojalá*, and drop our flowers into the running water.

They are red and gold. For a moment, like me, the water bursts into flames.

A. Kyce Bello is a writer, mother, nurse, herbalist, and the editor of this collection.

Elms and riverbank give way to an ever-widening river. Photograph by EC Ryan.

Every Day I Walk Along the River

Cynthia West

It is silver coin, rich with the rush
      of water over stones.

It is a feast of magpies slicing
      black and white ladders to the sun.

The warmth is not hidden behind clouds.
      As my feet crush brittle weeds, I smell roses,
      with bees drinking music until they fall.

Friends warn me not to go alone,
      but if they came, their talk would overwhelm
      the flutes in the rushes along the shore.

Every day I bring my red wagon to gather
      the secrets that bloomed in the night.
      There are loaves and apples, wine as well.

Cynthia West is known for her paintings, poetry, photography, digital imaging and book arts. Her home, where she has lived for thirty-five years with her family, is a healing center, studio, and gallery. She is the author of four collections of poetry: *For Beauty Way, 1000 Stone Buddhas, Rainbringer*, and *The New Sun*.

Imprints

Chrissie Orr

Find your place on the planet. Dig in and take responsibility from there.
— Gary Snyder

Once in his life a man ought to concentrate his mind upon the remembered earth.
He ought to give himself up to a particular landscape in his experience; to look at
it from as many angles as he can, to wonder upon it, and dwell upon it.
— N. Scott Momaday

You know, I think if people stay somewhere long enough — even white people —
the spirits will begin to speak to them. It's the power of the spirits coming from
the land. The spirits and the old powers aren't lost, they just need people to be
around long enough and the spirits will begin to influence them.
— Crow elder

May 21st 2007. *The pulsing sounds of the river are trying to tell me something. I strive to listen as I hope for answers. I search in vain for my friend's son that has gone on walkabout; he has his hiding places on the river. There was only a dead trout to be found. No clouds for the first time in a week. I planted purple heirloom tomatoes, butternut squash, eggplant, peppers and think about the differences of gardening here to when I tended the potatoes and turnips in the damp earth of Scotland. I have had to learn anew.*

For the past few days I have been walking with the Santa Fe River. It is only a mile from where I have settled. It is so close I feel its presence through the open doors. I can wander down the hill through the scattered piñon and juniper trees until I reach the sandy arroyo that leads me to the riverbed. This river meanders from its headwaters at Santa Fe Lake above Lake Peak in the Sangre de Cristo range for 46 miles to its confluence with the wide, brown Rio Grande. For most of the year it is a dry corridor, the rusted skeletons of old cars hold up its eroding banks, its trees struggle to push their roots deeper searching for lost moisture and its animals quietly disappear to other more nourishing habitats. This river, the arid heart of our community, was recently declared the nation's most endangered waterway!

It is the high desert here, water is not apparent in the landscape, we crave it, we constantly talk about it, we dam it, we carry around plastic bottles filled with spring water from other places yet we are thirsty all the time. We imagine it, we dream it lapping around our feet, between our toes and filling out our dry wrinkled skin.

This year we were blessed, it snowed and snowed, more snow than we have seen in a hundred years. The town virtually shut down for a day, as no one could get out of their driveways. It was hip deep. I nearly disappeared when taking the compost from the house to the garden. Now the abundant snowmelt and delicious soft spring rains have brought a new vibrant lush green. Not the usual olive brown green but a yellow tinged dancing green. The leaves on the trees are full. Dormant seeds have awoken in places that are usually desolate. We are rejoicing, the reservoir is, for the moment, full. So the city mothers and fathers have declared that for a few special weeks, the river can run. I wonder since when have humans had the right to determine the life of the river? Now the permission is given to open the floodgates and allow the river its freedom. So it flows through us carrying its stories, scattering its memories and connecting us again to others further south.

I am not from here, I am a native from another land, where the idea of a dry river is inconceivable, the colour green is different, I laugh in another language, I could be called an invasive species but the way I carefully choose to place one foot in front of another is the same as it has always been. These walks are my salvation, my rooting to this new and foreign place, my understanding, my contemplation, my sensing of place.

The river reflecting the sun. Photograph by EC Ryan.

May 23rd *The clouds have arrived again, more spring rains have soaked the earth. I do not remember a time when we had rains like this. They normally do not arrive until monsoon season in July and August. Last night there was a strong wind that blew through the open window and woke me. The peas are steadily throwing out their slender tendrils and producing pale white flowers. I think about what art means to those living up river compared to those living down river.*

I have a need to walk, I always have. I'm a mover I cannot be still. There is something in the repetitive motion that brings the stillness. I do not remember the exact time and place of my first unsteady steps, but I do remember the sensation of my feet touching the ground and I can still see the remains of their small imprints that were left in urban Scotland. As a child I walked everywhere. I walked back and forth to school, I walked to the centre of town, I walked to the burn to catch sticklebacks and I as awkwardly grew into my teenage years I walked to the local hangout coffee shops where we would meet boy friends, play billiards and listen to Dylan. Later, on moving to the big city of Edinburgh, I continued with my walking, from my flat at the bottom of the Royal Mile to my classes at the Art College and from there to the pub and home again.

My feet are layered and lined with memories.

The knowledge that gathered on my soles is of cobblestones, grey granite, dark moist earth, heather, moss and bracken, the salt seas, all penetrated into my being. These embedded patterns have been carried with me to the Northern New Mexico desert where I walk today along the living river. The old patterns merge with the new, that of water engraved mud and rock, prickles and wind blown hard red earth.

It is through the soles of my feet that I gain my sense of place and it is through my intuitive sensibility to place that my creativity emerges.

May 24th *Another rainstorm last night that brought in the cold air. A crow flew into the cities main transformer and blew out the power for a few hours. I worried about the crow. I headed upriver about three miles where the riverbed is narrow and passes through dense groves of cottonwoods. I wanted to check on the beavers. They had disappeared from the area and only came back a few years ago. They are doing so well that they have successfully dammed an area and created a new pond. From the soaked ground huge white daisies have surfaced. It sounds different here; it's the habitat of the red-winged black birds, which tend to stay upstream. Its time to water the garden, no rains today. The butternut squash are struggling; they have not yet adapted to their new environment. That always takes time.*

As I write these words in my studio many miles from my homeland, I feel my feet on the concrete floor, see the junipers and piñons sway in the spring winds but hear the sounds of seagulls. I live in a land that is not home.

Like the river there have been many twists and turns in my life. At times it has been dry and dormant and at other moments it has flowed with renewed energies and insights.

The first time I came to the Southwest was thirty years ago, just after the birth of my redheaded daughter. She was born by the water to the sound of bagpipes and the ships on the Clyde. Her father was an American I met in Edinburgh on one of my long walks. Being a native from the Southwest he had contacts here in New Mexico and after a year of back and forth letter writing and negotiations we were invited to Window Rock, the main town on the "rez," the local term for the Navajo reservation. The Navajo Nation, Diné Bikéyah, extends into the states of Utah, Arizona and New Mexico. It covers 27,000 square miles about the same size as Scotland with a population of 250,000 compared to 5,000,000! This was a totally foreign experience for me, a shock to my Scottish system. The openness and vast terrain made me uncomfortable and the red-brown dry earth hurt my feet. This was to be my first encounter with a dry riverbed; it was inconceivable. How could there be a river without water? I would wait for it to appear.

I could not comprehend.

This was not part of my vocabulary. I was a product of the compacted urban British environment, my experiences informed by narrow streets, crowds, tight spaces and short vistas. This rural expansive land was in complete contrast to my inherited patterns. The air felt different on my skin, the colours somehow too bright, the jagged touch of the earth cracked my skin. The sky was like I had never seen before, a new sort of bluish blue.

I placed my feet cautiously in front of one and other and walked to learn about the openness. The land began to show me its wonders.

I broke open.

May 25th *The grey blue dense clouds are back, moisture is again in the air, it feels more like Scotland than New Mexico. I think I am dreaming, not sure where I am. I write about here and there but wonder where I will land. I feel lost. It snowed in Taos two days ago. The river's current is stronger and has in places burst its banks. I found what looked like wild peas growing near the waters edge. A tornado warning has been issued for the rest of the early evening. The mysterious times continue.*

After Window Rock we returned to Scotland where I continued my love for moving around, a long-term community arts project on the Isle of Arran, travel and street performance in Turkey, murals in Isfahan, notoriety in Germany for creating wonders out of cardboard boxes and five years on the island of Corsica. It was not enough. I missed those vast horizons. I have been living back in the Southwest now for twenty years. It was that time on the "rez" that enticed me back here, its powerful essence remaining with me as I traveled and worked in Europe.

I moved to be in a place that opened me to new possibilities. I knew I would miss the familiarity of the Scottish mists; the sound of seagulls and the voices and laughter of my people but the pull back here was too strong.

I tried to settle in Albuquerque. The openness of the city made me feel vulnerable. I only stayed there three years until I migrated north. It was an important move; I have grown. I have widened my own internal horizons, expanded my vision and continued to learn. The openness has opened me and in turn has cracked open my visual understandings.

During these last twenty years I have continued to develop my work through the lessons of the landscape. Here I live on the land, I see the mountains, the juniper and piñI know where the sun rises and sets at different times of the year. I hear and feel the winds. I have the doors open most of the year to bring the inside out and the outside in.

I live with the land.

One cannot ignore the landscape here. You become part of it. My skin is a darker colour, my feet are coarse and hardened and formed to their new patterns. I still cannot say that I am from here, I am not sure when one can say they belong to a place. What does it take to feel that sense of belonging?

I only feel I belong when my feet touch the ground.

May 27th *The flowing current of the river pulls me. I have a need to be by the moving water. When I woke this morning it was still dark and there was one lone bird singing. I went to the river. Its banks are wet and muddy, it must have raged through this narrow space the other night bringing its power from the mountains. The main stream is much deeper, it has burst through its banks to form new side streams. The retreating water leaving its magic repeating patterns on the damp earth, my footsteps merge with them. The first orange yellow monarch butterfly hovers near me. I feel the delicateness of its wings. There has been a drought in Scotland, my mother said. She has been hand watering the garden. I do not have this as a memory.*

I am composing these words just days after having completed a visual arts project with youth in treatment. These kids were struggling to combat the effects of major drug and alcohol abuse, gang warfare, lack of love and too many numerous atrocities of our declining social system to mention. As part of the project process I taught them to take photographs as a means to document their surroundings, individual experiences and feelings as they related or did not relate to Peace.

A tricky endeavor.

It was intriguing to me that the most profound connection they had to this process was when I took them out of their usual setting in the treatment centre and up into the mountains or to walk the river. Some did not want to go too far, the wildness of nature being a little too overwhelming after the confines of the centre but even if they just took a few steps their attitude changed and they became alive. For one girl it was the first time I had seen her smile. They told me that their place of peace was with nature and for most of the time they had forgotten this important relationship.

Sculpture gallery in the river, near Canyon Road. Photograph by A. Kyce Bello.

We should never forget our intrinsic relationship with the earth and our natural instincts to feel its presence. As the world spins more and more out of control we will have to work harder to continue this relationship. We will have to remind each other to put our fingers in the earth and our feet in the rivers.

At this moment and place in time I feel this is my charge, to remind those that have forgotten. How I will continue to do this I am not sure, but somehow I have the notion that if I keep walking and flowing with the pulse river and learning from the natural patterns that surround me. If I keep my feet connected and my eyes open then there is a chance.

As the river reshapes itself to the ever-changing conditions of nature, so must our creative ideas shift and flow. This Santa Fe River has a huge story to share. It is up to us to listen.

May 28th *I followed the Rio Grande north to Taos. The river is full and running wild. At times flowing back over itself as it twists and swirls southwards. I imagine the moment when it meets with the calmer Santa Fe River that I am getting to know so well. I walked through the tall grasses crisscrossing the acequias in Ranchitos. I found more wild peas, milkweed and dusky pink honeysuckle. Such a different microclimate, huge cotton woods providing shade and shelter from the intense sun. Its softer, gentle, the birds are singing another song. It took me nine blows on the dandelion to disperse the seeds.*

Every morning I wake torn between the desire to save the world and
an inclination savor it. This makes it difficult to plan the day.
＿ E. B. White

～～

Artist and activist Chrissie Orr has created place and community based art in the name of social change all over the world. Her most recent project was El Otro Lado: The Other Side, an interdisciplinary community art installation in Santa Fe. She is the recipient of the Santa Fe 2009 Mayors Award for Excellence in the Arts.

River Voices, River Bodies

Nanda Currant

My love affair with rivers begins with my father, on trips in the high Sierras. He taught me to fish by hand, and to find the tiny shelves in a stream by sliding my hand under them to carefully catch the waiting trout. Sitting, often in silence, we cooked our meal, afterwards wandering farther upstream. We took many photos on our trips and I began to see in the darkroom the nuances of light that bounced off the river's surface.

Rivers need a healthy turbulence to survive and they need meanders and turns to express their passionate nature. If a river is dammed or channeled its life force is contained, it cannot regulate itself, and it loses its wisdom. As a dancer, I have learned to respond to the movement of my own river body through breath and micro movements that combine pulses and waves. This work for me has the same creative impetus as a river. As a dancer, my body needs the same freedom that a river needs to find balance. As an artist I am compelled to engage in my community, and to weave the arts and sciences into a passionate dialogue so doors open and relationships form to keep the outer and inner rivers flowing. What supports a vibrant river also applies to my movement and dance and creative heart.

For me, this convergence has taken the form of performance art created on behalf of river ecologies. This work has given me the chance to bring nature to life and to engage the community in creative expression as a part of the natural world so that ordinary citizens can harness their ability to protect a valued resource while strengthening their relationship with the river. Performance art offers the greater community a chance to remember who they are in the big sense of their lives and to revisit what nature holds for them. The river lies mute until we hear its voice and attend to its story.

We have a Canyon Road in Santa Fe filled with artistic voices, but we need vital canyons and streams or else art remains merely a reference to what was once the Southwest. The landscape and culture of the Santa Fe River are what brought people here. It is ironic at best if, in our emphasis on the arts and what inspires the impetus to create, we do not protect the mythic voice of the land and restore and protect the environment.

Inherent in the substance and story of the river are rich themes that forge themselves out of the many elements that enliven our senses along its banks. The history of mankind is carried by the river, and lives in the rushes along its banks. For as long as humans have lived in proximity to rivers, we have listened to their stories in order to create our own. The natural world tells a tale of animals, land, and river, guiding us in our lives. We need to re-story place, and the river, because in a very real sense, its story is our story. If we plan to keep traveling this river, and to be nurtured by it, we must be prepared to benefit nature as well as ourselves.

I cannot imagine separating art from nature, or community from the beauty that sustains life. It is not enough for me to simply draw what I love and frame it; I want nature's story engaged in the community. I want to see large groups of people express themselves in performances where they can connect to the life story of the river.

A river is a keystone in the environment; the life surrounding a river depends on its active vitality. The Santa Fe River still remembers its birthright. It pulses during a hard rainfall, filling with runoff that briefly renews, feeds, and shapes the ecosystem. The river speaks, saying, "Here I am, still filled with secrets, with new life, and with possibility."

By paying attention to our dreams, we make it possible for animals, rivers, and plants to appear, asking us for aid. I believe this is part of an ecological imagination that seeps into and through us. Can we listen? The interconnectedness of all life is integral to our creative spirit. Our imagination will run as dry as our rivers if we do not take an interest as artists and community members in the natural world and the cries and whispers of the river.

⌇⌇⌇

Artist, therapist, and educator Nanda Currant has facilitated community performances undertaken on behalf of river ecosystems. She is the author of *Riverworks: Performance and Community Art for Rivers* and *Bringing Nature to Life: The Use of Performance Art for Environmental Restoration.*

The river in winter. Photograph by A. Kyce Bello.

Poem in the River

James McGrath

I found a poem in the river.

It gurgled, sputtered around a stone
    trying to dry itself.

There were words sparkling
    in the eddies of the current,
    scrambled words edged with rounded vowels
    the color of sunrise crowning the water.

I tossed a sheet of paper into the river.
    It swirled, catching the scent of mint
    and the broken twigs of an early winter.

I wanted to bring the river poem
    home in a jar, but the water tumbled
    into a canyon and turned into a voice
    that stole the words from the reflection of clouds.

I knew the river flowed into the sea
    mixing the tongues of the world
    into the poem I was seeking.

Somewhere behind me, a magpie was reciting
    a nursery rhyme using all the words
    hidden in his nest.

Tomorrow I will sit on the stone
    in the river memorizing that
    magpie's rhyme.

~~~

Poet and artist James McGrath hosts annual poetry readings in his orchard along the Santa Fe River in La Cieneguilla. He is the author of three collections of poetry: *At the Edgelessness of Light,* *Speaking With Magpies,* and *Dreaming Invisible Voices.*

Running Dry
Staci Matlock
The Santa Fe New Mexican
November 9, 2003

This article brings us up to date on the river's political life over the last couple of decades. As it shows, efforts to renew the river's flow and to protect its eroding bed have been ongoing, but with little effect.

The powerful river that runs through Santa Fe's history has long been choked off, and decades of discussion and millions of dollars have not restored the flow.

After 20 years of good intentions and millions of taxpayer dollars, Santa Fe has failed to restore a regular flow of water down to the Santa Fe River, a goal touted in several City Different plans.

Growing population, increased water use and drought leave the once year-round river dry most of the time.

The lack of water raises questions about whether this is still a river or just an arroyo where the city dumps its storm water and residents dump their trash.

Putting water back in the river is complex—not because of cost but because it involves getting some two-dozen government agencies, city and county departments, commissions and advocacy groups to agree on restoring flow.

The biggest problem, river advocates say, is the lack of will to do it.

Mark Wood, chairman of the seven-member Santa Fe River Commission, resigned in frustration two weeks ago because of the lack of progress.

"Only through a living river can the above-ground and below-ground water supplies be sustainable," he said. "The river needs to be included in an overall water budget. Without it, the city has cut its own throat."

A River Grows a Town

" La creciente, la creciente," the children of Agua Fria shouted as they ran toward the banks of the Santa Fe River to watch a flash flood rampage through the village, carrying animals, trees, and cars.

Ramon Romero, president of Agua Fria Water Association and Agua Fria Village Association, remembers joining the dash to the riverbanks from the time he was six years old in the 1950s. Stories of the river run through his family for three centuries back. He grew up hearing of a time when the river filled nearby ponds and flowed along acequias to water crops.

Historians say when Pedro de Peralta chose Santa Fe as the new capital of Spain's New Mexico province in 1609, it was because of the river. A Spanish merchant more than a century later described the river water as "crystalline clear." Duck ponds sparkled, trout jumped, and tall cottonwoods grew along the riverbanks.

More than 200 years later, the water flowing in the river dwindled to a trickle in 1947 when the city began building dams to serve the growing population of Santa Fe. When the reservoirs were full, water flowed again in the river. In times of drought, the downstream agricultural users in Agua Fria went thirsty and the river went dry.

Chamisa and old farm equipment grow along the river near Frenchy's Field. Photograph by EC Ryan.

Now 52, Romero rides his Arabian gelding, Rojo, almost daily in the sandy riverbed. He gallops past banks eroded 12 feet deeper in the last dozen years by storm-water runoff and gravel operations. In places, the riverbed looks like a landfill.

As the bank erodes, residents use pieces of concrete, trees, and old cars to shore up the sides and keep their property from sliding downstream in flash floods.

With or without water, it is still a river in Romero's mind. "That is my memory of it. But to people who have no memory of it, who didn't grow up here, they may see it as an arroyo."

Strangling a River

David Coss, city councilor and former city public-works director, said he overhears Santa Fe visitors commenting on the sad condition of the river.

"They are shocked, or confused, or befuddled, when they see the river. They want to know why it's so dry," said Coss, who works for the State Land Office. "It is a question we all need to ask." The city has spent $5.4 million for river-channel improvements in the past eight years, according to the finance department.

Another $149,000 in state-grant funds were devoted to the river in that period. Most of the money—$4million—was allocated between 1997 and 1999. The city has spent less on the river in the past two years—$5,000 last year and $49,000 this year.

But the money spent was aimed at fixing erosion problems, not restoring flow, in spite of repeated official city resolutions and plans calling for the river's revival.

"There's no commitment, regardless of what's on paper, to bring the river back to life," Wood said.
The Santa Fe River bed runs along a 46-mile path from the Sangre de Cristo mountain range to its final union with the Rio Grande. A 285-acre watershed of roads, arroyos, springs, and hillsides drains into the riverbed.

Mature cottonwoods died as the city plugged leaks in the reservoirs and drought dried the land. Siberian elms took over.
As the number of paved city streets and commercial parking lots grew, so did the amount of storm water pouring off the pavement and cutting into the river channel, exposing gas, water and sewer lines.

"Without water, there is no river," said Paige Grant, executive director of the Santa Fe Watershed Association, quoting the mantra of river advocates.

In September 1995, the City Council unanimously approved the Santa Fe River Corridor Master Plan. It listed steps for creating a natural recreational destination along the river from Two Mile Reservoir to the city's wastewater-treatment plant by 2000 at an estimated cost of $8 million.

A volunteer task force spent months coming up with the half-inch-thick document, which cited earlier plans dating to 1985 that aimed to restore the river. It called for a river project coordinator at the city and creation of the Santa Fe River Commission.
Ron Sandoval served as the city's river coordinator for more than five years, but he resigned last year and the position remains unfilled.

"We've really accomplished very little, and it is such a talented group," said Wood, who was appointed to the Santa Fe River Commission in 2001. The group's well-researched suggestions seem to stall when they reach city departments, he said.

Good Ideas, No Takers

For more than two decades, retired engineer Ted Williams has been proposing a solution to the Santa Fe River's lack of water. He suggests building pipelines along public roads and pumping some of the city's treated effluent back up to the old Two Mile Reservoir. The amount piped would keep vegetation alive and recharge the city's aquifer without hurting the water flow to people downstream of the treatment plant, he claims.

"In the old days, I was paid well for good ideas and it was easy to sell them," said Williams, who has designed water systems for other states and countries. "Now I have a good idea and I can't give it away."

A 1999 Santa Fe Water Management and River Restoration Strategy, approved by the City Council and used to help obtain federal funding, talks about using treated effluent in the river.

Councilor Miguel Chavez chaired the Wastewater Reuse Task Force that included Williams. The main problem with piping the treated effluent up to Two Mile Reservoir is cost, Chavez said.

Another effluent-reuse plan unanimously approved by the Santa Fe River Commission a year ago sits in some city department, Wood said.

Hard data show that water flowing downriver, regardless of where it came from, will benefit Santa Fe—especially under a relatively new state law that rewards cities for recharging aquifers, Wood said. "We can show again and again that increasing the flow in the river increases the net gain in water (in the aquifer)," he said.

Ron Sandoval remembers the "big ugly," a massive lump of concrete built by the Army Corps of Engineers to stop severe erosion under a sewer line near St. Francis Drive and West Alameda Street. It cost the city a couple of million dollars to make the mess prettier.

Sandoval grew up in the neighborhood, back when only addicts, drug dealers and fools hung out around the river between Camino Alire and St. Francis Drive. Now a park attracts families to stroll along the Santa Fe River's banks — even though the waterway is mostly dry.

Connecting people to the river is crucial if they are to care about it, Sandoval said.

In the past few years, the city has successfully restored native vegetation and controlled erosion along some river reaches. Tall concrete check dams near the Guadalupe Church have been reduced in height and replaced with shallow drops that slow the rush of water during storms, creating small pools where water percolates underground and helps nearby vegetation. Local people and schoolchildren in two programs started by Sandoval did much of the work.

"In erosion control, I think we've done fairly well," said councilor Chavez, a member of the team that wrote the corridor master plan. "We've done well in some areas (of river restoration) and not so well in others."

Beyond the City

Sandoval is now a county projects manager. The county's next river-restoration project, expected to begin in two months, is improving a stretch from San Ysidro River Park to Lopez Lane, the site of extensive erosion.

The Santa Fe Watershed Association obtained a $300,000 grant to pay for engineering the project, and the design was created for free by a graduate student. The county and the Trust for Public Land are negotiating with four private individuals who own land in and along the river to buy their property.

Downstream, where the riverbed flattens out above the treatment plant, is a State Land Office project Sandoval helped complete. Willows and cottonwoods, barely sticks when they were planted, show healthy growth despite the drought.

Sandoval says it will take 15 years for the river to flow again. Chavez is skeptical it will ever flow. Williams and Wood believe it could flow in a couple years if the city changed its approach.

Coordination between city and county departments and other entities remains key to restoring the Santa Fe River.

"The river needs to be deemed worthy enough to have a certain amount of water dedicated to it," Wood said. "It will take the community demanding from the administration that the river be a priority."

Coss Agrees.

"If we can't have a living river, then I don't think we have a sustainable future as a community," he said.

Paired images showing river narrowing over time below downtown Santa Fe. This image was taken in 1936 by the USDA Forest Service. Agua Fria St. runs parallel to the river, and arroyo Torreón enters the river from the north.

The same location in 1951. Camino Alire now crosses the Santa Fe River. Image by the City of Santa Fe.

By 2005, urban density had overwhelmed the river, constricting its course considerably while vastly increasing the amount of floodwater channeled into it. Image by the City of Santa Fe.

Places on the Santa Fe River

Miriam Sagan

1. Randall Davey Audubon Center

Walled garden set
Among dry red hills.

Fountain, a simple stone
Bubbles over —

Talking water
Out of the living rock,

Hummingbird,
Black orange-tipped wing butterfly,

Yellow butterfly on a field of lavender,
Yarrow.

Like any Impressionist
I sit on the bench in my straw hat:

Creation is born
Of name and water.

2. Cerro Gordo

The child says:
"A river, sometimes
it has water in it,
sometimes it doesn't..."

Not the rivers
I grew up with
But my daughter, born here,
Thinks of river
As dry course.

River did cut this canyon.
Wear down rock
Riddled with ancient shells
Mementoes of a sea
Long ebbed away.

The poet Phil,
Zen priest,
Lived in the little temple here
By Cerro Gordo Park,
Stupa properly situated
Between a turtle-shaped hill
And a river. He used to say:
"One day
we'll just turn on the faucet
and sand will pour out..."

And once, when the kids were little,
My friend Hope and I
Scrambled down the bank
Took them hobo-ing
Along the weedy track
Until we tripped an electronic eye
Heard the canned voice warn:
GET BACK, GET BACK,
THE POLICE WILL BE CALLED.
We hadn't realized this way
Was anyone's private property.

3. Alameda

At the corner of Palace and Alameda
There is a *descansos*
For JJ Vigil
Who hung, or swung
Into sheer space from the bridge
And died —
Memorialized
By plastic blue hydrangeas,
An American flag,
Bouquets of grief and remembrance.

A little farther upstream, at the corner
To the turn
To Atalaya School
My daughter and I saw each morning
A llama and a donkey,
And we'd sing out—llama!
Pronouncing it correctly
The totem animals
For each day's elementary.

What is the source of my water?
Reservoir, and should it fail
The wells.
Decade of drought
Has coated my tea kettle
With residue of hard water,
Scum of minerals.
What is the source of my water?
Body, rain, memory, dream.

4. Alto Street

spiderweb
on the mailbox
still waiting

half tame sparrows
the house cat
watches

blue circle—slash—line
O'Keeffe painted blind
hand set on canvas

bad news
from everywhere—
what's for supper?

slow stars
above my house
year after year

even the memory
has begun to fade
hazy moon

moonstones
wrapped away—
like a forgotten dream

midnight loud crickets
still no sound
of the key in the lock

rain catches me—
I stayed too long
gossiping

sweeping the dust
under the rug
she writes a poem

Sand river. Photograph by EC Ryan.

5. Justice Department Santa Fe Internment Camp

A Maxfield Parish sky
Hill overlook
A courting couple sits
He, long-haired and dark, perches
On the granite boulder
That marks the Japanese internment camp.
She, bleached blonde and pierced,
Says: I come here all the time
But I've never read the marker
All the way through.
He looks at the long view of the city
Says—What happened? Did somebody die?
Sunset pinks the Jemez to the west,
Below, we find the red roof
Of St. Anne's, blocks from our house,
Upriver, the campanile
Of the Bataan Memorial Building.

Footprints, bird tracks, anthills
Ephemeral as haiku
Wind writing on sand
there's nothing left but dust,
Those memories.
And somehow, we've been remiss.
In the new suburban neighborhood
Split-levels lit with fairy lights at solstice
Or equinox's candled Jack-o-Lanterns.
Land rolls down to the river,
The Feed Lot, the laundromat, pizzeria, and a place for chai.
Along the banks, sculptures
Lift stars or airplanes high
Above the bear claw grasp of time.
Footbridges cross, no water beneath.
Heavens roll to the abyss.

6. Frenchy's Field

Water doesn't flow through the dry river
Water carves the land, leaves a wadi, an arroyo, a wash
Water can lift up your house and carry it away
On its feet of flash flood

Water composes most of my body
Is colorless, tastes of the end of thirst
Water in glasses, common, critiqued
Ask for it without ice, with lemon, in bottles
As if it weren't already rare and precious
All day we ask ourselves and everyone else — will it rain?
Water consoles me with its tears
Water is in my name
Miriam's Well, a source of water in the desert
That follows us like a shadow, an angel, a mother
With a watering can
This water from an unseen source
No hydrologist can find
Only a prophet
I came from a place with water
And I knew nothing about it
Now I know it takes a shape
From any cupped hand

7. San Ysidro Crossing

sunflowers, purple peas
two white cabbage moths
sky gone cumulous
stone ledge, lizard
swale

what's dry wash,
passable, or waterfall
what designates the name
trash heap, or river —
saint's prayer,
rain.

Miriam Sagan is the author of over twenty books, including her most recent collection of poetry, *Map of the Lost*, and a memoir, *Searching for a Mustard Seed: A Young Widow's Unconventional Story*. She is the director of the creative writing program at the Santa Fe Community College.

A Walk to the River

Seth Biderman

A childhood friend of mine grew up, settled Back East, and returned to Santa Fe for a summer visit with a big-eyed, two-year old son named Moses. I asked Moses if he'd like to see the Santa Fe River down below my house. Moses, who'd spent an afternoon or two watching Harvard kids row along the Charles, ran a few circles in the yard as a way of accepting my invitation and started picking up stones. Splash! he said. Splash in the water!

This was a problem. It hadn't rained in weeks. If the Santa Fe River was flowing it was doing so three feet below its rock and sand surface. But Moses was already heading out the yard, and my friend and I had little choice but to follow.

He rambled down the street, pretending to throw the stones and making his splashing noise. I confessed to my friend, in an underhanded adult tone of voice, that the river wasn't exactly flowing. He laughed. He was used to fatherhood and not so concerned about dashing young Moses' illusions. But I had just met Moses and was anxious to make a good impression lest he forever associate me with fickle junior high girls and carob chip cookies and other sources of heartbreak. I glanced up toward the Sangre de Cristos hoping there'd be an unseasonable cloudburst—some sort of post-global warming la niña effect, maybe—but the mountains were crisp against the blue June sky.

Moses, I called after him. This isn't such a big river.

He looked up at me, spit out a few splashes, and rambled on.

It isn't far from my house to the Santa Fe River. When it rains hard in August I'll pull on my hiking boots, don a poncho, and walk down to listen. The brown water rumbles past, cutting at the banks, and I wonder if it might flood one day. I've heard that the Santa Fe River used to jump its banks, now and again; that just before I was born, it flooded clear across West Alameda and lapped the doorsteps of the houses in the neighborhood across the street. I recall those TV reports about innocent folks in the Midwest losing their homes to the Mississippi, and I tell myself I should look into purchasing flood insurance. Then the rain stops, the water sinks away, and I walk back up to my house, uneasily reassured.

Moses ploughed onward. He was a pretty good walker, for a two year old. He leaned his torso forward and swung the splashing stones around in his hands and let his feet figure out how to keep up. We cut into the abandoned chamisa and ragweed field that leads to the river. I stopped and pointed out an impressive hill of red ants but Moses kept walking.

Boys playing in water above check dam. Photograph by EC Ryan.

There was a time when he could've splashed his stones in the Santa Fe River. When he got older, he could've navigated a Kmart lake raft down the Santa Fe River, snapping the blue plastic oars on shopping carts, bruising his knees on the bottom rocks, dragging the deflating thing back up to Patrick Smith Park to do it again. He could've splashed Santa Fe River water on squealing ten-year-old girls during birthday picnics. The Santa Fe River could've served as a wet no man's land for his Capture the Flag games; it could've stood silent witness when he and his junior high friends stole a forbidden sip of beer.

That was then.

My friend and I picked up our pace and arrived at the bank's edge with Moses, in time to watch him take it all in: The wide sandy flat. The scattering of embedded stones. Steeply eroded banks. Dying elms, stunted cottonwoods. Exposed concrete drainage pipes.

My friend knelt down beside Moses.

See there, kid? It's a sand river.

Moses nodded. A sand river, he said.

My friend helped his son down the bank, and I watched the two of them throw stone after stone into the dry riverbed. A tiny explosion of sand popped up around the stones when they hit. When Moses timed his splashing noise right, it was almost like the Santa Fe River was flowing again, snow-melted water splashing up, swallowing Moses' stones, and gurgling onward, in perfect meander. Then I opened my eyes, and the river was gone again.

~cc~

Born and raised in Santa Fe, Seth Biderman lives with his wife just above the south bank of the Santa Fe River. He is a graduate of the Master´s in Writing Program at UNM, and is a teacher in the Santa Fe Public Schools.

Houses, mountains, and riverbed as seen from pedestrian bridge near Frenchy's Field. Photograph by EC Ryan.

Under the Road

Angelo Jaramillo

There is a tunnel emanating from the northwest end of Alto Park that juts into The Santa Fe River. During our last year of elementary school a cohort of us religiously ventured down there. We entered the tunnel's entrance, but never went any further. The tunnel reeked of everything from stale alcohol to dead animals to rotten feces. It maintained dimensionless radiance, decrepit magnificence. From a distance the entrance to the tunnel looked dark, fathomless, open and destitute like a prostitute's wretched pursed lips prepared to suck bottomless smoke. Upon closer inspection, the tunnel near the entrance possessed streaming bars of light reflected off concrete. I couldn't tell if it was a sewer tunnel or water tunnel or drainage tunnel or what the difference was.

We heard all kinds of rumors about the tunnel. We heard there was no exit. We heard there was an exit. We were told by some older kids who hung around the neighborhood that in order to get to the exit you had to walk through tunnel for miles, stoop through tunnel for more miles, and then crawl through the tunnel for even more miles. These same people told us there was a fork in the tunnel after you had walked through it for an indeterminate distance. If you chose the wrong way you would never be able to return to where you veered off. One neighborhood kid warned us that several kids a few years back attempted to explore the tunnel through the city. They ended up trapped inside. Part of the tunnel had collapsed. Nobody could come in time to rescue them. The tunnel apparently ran throughout the entire city.

Undeterred by these veiled admonitions, we decided to venture down the tunnel's mythological innards. On a foray into the interior of the tunnel, we became progressively excited. We wanted to explore more of what the tunnel didn't have to offer. Five of us spent a week politicking our idea around the playground at Gonzales Elementary, and were able to recruit three girls. We walked from school, a group of eight, entering the Santa Fe River closer to St. Francis Drive, walking through the dry, bromidic corridor, pebbles, rocks, and petite boulders littering soft sandy skin pockmarked with dead weeds, old tires, scraps of rusted metal, rusty nails, and shards of beer-bottle glass. At the entrance of the tunnel, our smiles, our laughter, our joviality, our innocence vanished like shadows from sunsets. We looked at each other. Johnny grabbed the flashlight from Greg and entered the tunnel. Johnny was the leader. I followed immediately followed by Nathan, Anita, Virginia, Jessica, and Miguel, with Greg picking-up the tail. The tunnel echoed intimately pushing warm breath back into brusque faces, deafening our congested eardrums. It smelled like temperate solid waste. It was dark with the exception of light passing through bars of overhead ventilation gates. A rivulet of shit and urine and water ran through the center of the tunnel. Rambunctious flies everywhere. The girls giggled, gagged, and screeched. The guys up front and in back talked trash about how far they'd ventured through the tunnel and about how unafraid they were. The four flashlights covered the front and rear.

Decorated pipe draining into the Santa Fe River. Photograph by EC Ryan.

Based on calculations from a reconnoitering expedition a week earlier, we recognized we were standing directly under St. Francis Drive. The roaring tumult of cars passing overhead shook inner walls of tunnel. The roof seemed ready to cave-in on every pass. The three girls immediately wanted to turn away. They giggled no longer. They became worried. Johnny fell back, handed the flashlight to me and said he would escort the girls out. He said he had been pretty far in the tunnel before. "When you get to the fork you need to make sure you veer right instead of left, otherwise you might get lost." I watched Johnny and the girls make their way toward the dim circle of light that became the entrance. The volume of cheer rose while they skipped and jogged their way out the body of the tunnel. They were safe again in the bosom of the dirty Santa Fe River where water was cool when water permeated. When the river ran, it was brown and always freezing. Soft sifting mud squished between toes, gripping for gravity beneath scant currents brushing naked calve muscles along the way to indeterminateness. Mexican looking chickabiddies splashed brown water over makeshift assembled rock and stick dam. This is when the rumble in the river would begin. Kids smashing kids with hard splashes, dunking one another in deep gathering pool beneath the dam, holding the head of the victim underneath the surface of water long enough to produce a bubble of ascending breath sporadically until a parent intervened. We had fun. In our neighborhood only the Mexican kids would swim in the dirty river. We learned how to bathe in unclean water. We breathed carbon fumes of passing automobiles speeding down West Alameda St. above our heads. Streams of polluted dark oily type substances waded down the riverbed surrounding sullied *shortes* stuck to naked bodies. We laughed and cheered and praised God for having something else to do other than waste our time. We loved and learned how to love through mischief and delinquency. The river belonged to us. There was no such thing as environmental development along the riverbed. There was no concept or implementation thereof pertaining to any sense of improvement projects. The Santa Fe River was an abandoned dumping ground for Hispanics that populated the neighborhood and a sanctuary for their kids and the homeless. We were wetbacks playing through dirty muddy water in the Santa Fe River.

For another mile or so we periodically felt and heard cars overhead. With every step further into pitch-black nowhere voices stopped chattering, breathing became burdensome, heat turned insufferable. Sweat splashed periodic puddles of various liquid substances beneath prudent steps. Flashlight beams bounced unsteadily against gray walls and graffiti art. The walls appeared to close in on us the further we stretched. The air was tighter, condensed, and thick. We had no idea where we were headed or how far we had come. The tunnel transmogrified into the Santa Fe River, a congruent transubstantiation. The unfriendly wind unexpectedly rushed upon us from the rear with fierce coldness dampening our clothes. Every now and then Miguel would insinuate that perhaps we should turn back. Greg punched him in the shoulder in reply.

We were determined to be the only kids in Santa to traverse the Santa Fe River tunnel for as far as physiology would allow. I asked Nathan to take the lead. A few steps ahead we discovered the fork in the tunnel. We deliberated for a while as to which tunnel we should take. A few weeks ago, when discussing tunnel adventures with some older kids from the neighborhood, one of the fellows informed us that the left tunnel leads to the Heaven & Hell tunnels near Rosario Cemetery. If any of us chose the Hell tunnel of the pair it was guaranteed we would be abducted for purposes of human sacrifice, never to return to earthly existence. We moved right. Shortly thereafter, the tunnel funneled into a smaller shaft.

Car parked on the Santa Fe River. Photograph by EC Ryan.

There was no turning around. The other end of the tunnel sustained vacuous magnetism, like staring into the blazing sun's oversight. We bent hips allowing backs to run parallel with circular ceiling. We were glad dimensions shifted. It was new territory. Our eagerness rejuvenated. We were determined to fulfill our dangerous experiment. We picked-up pace. We noticed walls around us were not covered in graffiti. There were no signs of discarded bottles or clothing. The dirty stream of water thinned. A car zoomed across our backs every once in awhile to remind us we were still somewhere near the whorish semblance of civilization. Eventually zooms ceased. Silence was present. The heat increased. We walked stooped over for who knows how long but it was much further than the distance we covered through the first section of tunnel when we were able to stand erect. The heat increased. The air thickened. The echoes that kept us company earlier disappeared. An omnipresent foreboding of realization overtook us. At any moment we could be trapped in the tunnel if the walls collapsed or if water were to rush through the center of space. We came upon a small angular tunnel on the side of one of the walls. I was selected by a vote of three to one to venture up the small tunnel to see what it was and where it led. We secretly hoped for an exit. I crawled up the tunnel about twenty feet to discover a corrugated gate. I could see trees and rocks and a segment of the sky. The sky was gray. It was drizzling outside. My eyes quickened. The air was refreshing. I breathed and breathed and breathed again and again. I didn't want to leave the spot. The others were yelling from below. Eventually Greg climbed up the side tunnel and started pulling my leg. We both came back to the reality of our dilemma. We all wanted to turn around. It wasn't fun anymore. We were suffocating, claustrophobic, delusional. I was starting to feel dizzy and weak. So were the others. Perhaps there lay an exit, the exit we had hoped for and heard about. The side tunnel was a clear indication that an exit was nearby. We agreed to venture further. The headlights of Miguel and Greg's flashlights began to wane and flicker. Shortly thereafter the batteries in their flashlights died. The prospects seemed discouraging. We moved forward cautiously, exhausted, obese with adrenaline.

The Santa Fe River was a forbidden place. As a young child growing up in Torreon Neighborhood we were not allowed to cross the Santa Fe River. Water hardly runs through the river, which is why this drainage tunnel remained a mystery. The tunnel was a relic of days gone by when storm water would actually run through the tunnel and empty into the Santa Fe River. My mother warned me not to go into the tunnel. If for some reason there was a heavy rainstorm the tunnel would fill to the brim with water and flood anyone that happened to be in there. I now recalled both my mother and father telling me tales of homeless people washed away by the storm water and found many days later when the stink of mortified corpse hit the surface. I recalled these heart-sunken tales bent over, trudging long distance into darkness. La Llorona was rumored to roam the Santa Fe River and every dark crevice and resting place in proximity around dusk, searching for her highly belated post-mortem victimless children she plundered beneath a river body. Needless to say these reminiscences didn't help assuage surmounting fears and anxiety. Everybody wanted to quit but nobody wanted to be the quitter. We said nothing to one another. We couldn't even really see or determine where each of us stood at the moment. After two flashlights burnt out we shifted one of the remaining two flashlights being utilized up front to the rear. The center of our four-man line became hazy, eliciting faint drafts of clothing moving inconspicuously through momentum of human body in desperate motion. Despite thickness of air and intensity of heat we moved rapidly through the second segment of tunnel with backs hunched over. The tunnel kept twisting, turning, and squirming frequently. There was no sense of direction. We felt we didn't know where we were any longer. There was no point of reference of place and time. We had been traveling through the tunnel for many hours.

Our pace slackened, nearly festooning to a standstill. All we could sense were the pair of sneakers ahead of us and head of hair behind us. We crawled, scraping elbows, knees, ankles, and shins. The concrete was much thicker. Echoes thudded against re-enforced stalwart walls. Further and further down the crawl space the tunnel thinned out again and again until the concrete was pushing down smeared backs. The sidewalls brushed wickedly against ribs. There was hardly any air left to breathe. Breaths became curt, frantic. Sweat billowing maniacally from brow and back of neck. Crawling was no longer an option. We tugged and pulled ourselves forward. A rumbling zoom wrecked our backs. We tugged and pulled and scraped knees wanting to get closer to the presumed exit that would rescue agony from reality. It stunk. The smell of sewer water, urine, and death pounded from the front. A garter snake slithered around our bodies in darkness causing a rush of yells and screamed expletives. It felt smooth, fast, and chill. I banged my head on the low ceiling. I couldn't maneuver my body in any way. We were trapped. The last flashlight flickered. We stopped. Nathan banged the flashlight with his palm. The flicker steadied. We pulled a few feet more. Nathan stopped. He was silent. For a long time now, several miles and many hours, we had not encountered any signs of human contact with the inner sanctum of the tunnel. Throughout the walking portion of the tunnel there was writing and scrawls covering the walls and ceiling. There were bottles, cigarette butts, and litter sporadically strewn throughout the tunnel. Through the mid-section where we crouched there was nothing but blank walls and displaced signs of facile water. Nathan could not move. He made a difficult turn on his side to show me what it was he saw in front of him. I pulled myself on my side to the front. Nathan handed me the light. Maggots chewed torn flesh ambitiously from a bird's exposed skeleton. A torn rag soaked in dirty water and blood was tied around the carcass. The bird was decomposing. Segments of rotting skeleton oozed corpulent stink that made me gag. Satanic messages and warnings scribbled the walls: "You will Die," "Turn Back...Now," and "Witness the Beast." A large picture of a goat head devil with prominent piercing conflagrated eyes rested above us. Despair could be surmised behind and ahead of us. Nathan flashed the light beyond the dead. Strewn piles consisting of besmirched clothes filtered the tunnel in front of us. A half-pint of Jack Daniels half filled rested against one of the sides of the tunnel. I was growing faint and weak very fast. Nathan gulped a swig from the bottle of Jack. Nathan threw up. Greg pissed in his pants. I was gagging voraciously. Profound zoom shimmied above our backs. The tunnel shook. Greg began to back out of the small tunnel space followed by Nathan and me. We couldn't turn around. We crawled backwards out of the small tunnel. It was methodical, monotonous, morose movement. Miguel was waiting for us at the change in dimension. A frozen statue on bended knee, tears cascading down flushed cheeks. He said he felt a cold breeze pass him while he was waiting for us alone. He led the way out of the second segment, hunched over. We stepped as rapidly as we could manage hunched over. The echoes behind us grew louder and closer. A stream of quick flashing effusion overtook us in the opposite direction. We yelled and screamed and laughed hysterically all the way out the tunnel leaping into the dry dead sandy bed of the Santa Fe River.

Street runoff cuts through debris in order to reach the river. Photograph by EC Ryan.

Angelo Jaramillo is the author of *The Darker: Tales of a City Different* and *Psalms of Anarchy*, published by Sunstone Press in Santa Fe. Jaramillo is a native born and raised Santa Fesino, stage and film actor, and educator. He is currently at work on his next book *Alcaldeza: The Life and Tragedy of Debbie Jaramillo*.

Channel incision below Caja del Oro Grant Road. Photograph by Tara Plewa.

River's Flow Done for Now
City Cuts Water Until Monsoons
John T. Huddy
Journal North
June 2, 2004

These early summer reports announcing the end of the river's brief season are, it seems, a tradition. Each year they appear, a few weeks or months after the initial announcement of snowmelt rushing through the river, signaling that anyone who hasn't yet gone fishing or wading had better hurry to the water while it still flows.

A river used to run through it.

But now the Santa Fe River—which has been running uncharacteristically full of late—is mostly dry once again.

After several weeks of creating a flowing river through town, city water engineers have decided to stop releasing water into the river from the city's Nichols and McClure reservoirs.

During the spring, Santa Fe's reservoirs nearly overflowed, thanks to above average snow-pack runoff from the Sangre de Cristo Mountains.

But with snow-pack runoff done for the summer, and another several weeks before New Mexico's monsoon season starts, keeping the reservoirs full for summer drought relief is critical and takes priority over releasing more water into the river, city reservoir supervisor Gary Martínez said.

"You have to make choices—do you want to release it or drink it?" Martínez said. "One thing we need is to store this water for the summer, because we don't know whether we'll need to use it or not."

The rare high flows the past several weeks had Santa Feans enjoying long dormant river activities, such as kayaking and even fishing, after the river was stocked with trout for the city's commUNITY Days festival last month.

Local environmentalists and members of the Santa Fe Watershed Association want city officials to devise a way to keep the river flowing more often.

They have recruited Santa Fe City Councilor David Coss to their cause.

In a recent Journal interview, Coss said he was helping draft a resolution calling for flow in the Santa Fe River at least nine months of the year.

By keeping the river flowing, Coss and fellow environmentalists maintain it not only keeps residents happy but helps recharge Santa Fe's aquifer.

But unless the summer monsoon season brings Santa Fe heavy rainfall—enough to cause the reservoir overflow—Martínez said keeping the Santa Fe River wet is not a likely scenario.

In the Season of Subtraction

Barbara Rockman

If I prostrate myself on a bed
of bent reeds and leaf vellum
I will imprint upon, no,
the shore will imprint me. Bosque
of burnt letters and unfilled bowls.
The river runs its absent current.
Shoal of gilt pages, cracked earth
and a three-pronged twig.

In the synagogue, supplicants
yearning toward the Book of Life
lay themselves in carpeted aisles, forehead to floor.
While I press against autumn's heart, the cottonwood's
spade-shaped leaves flip and flail caught in the cells of salt cedar.
How sad we might become in stillness.

Around my ankles, a strangle of dry grasses.
Around the fencepost, a twine of rust.
Along the river's edge, bird shadow, but no song.

Barbara Rockman teaches poetry at the Santa Fe Community College, Renesan Institute for Lifelong Learning, and in private workshops. Her work has appeared in numerous journals and the anthologies *Another Desert: Jewish Poets of New Mexico* and *Looking Back to Place*. Her collection of poems, *Sting and Nest*, is forthcoming from Sunstone Press.

///

Resurgence

Our strength lies in our imagination,
and paying attention
to what sustains life,
rather than what destroys it.

— Terry Tempest Williams

The Return of the River

Victoria Edwards Tester

It might be ridiculous that the sweet Mother of God could love us.
Or answer a prayer like that, when she does nothing
except appear sometimes when the wind blows
the horse brush in Skeleton Canyon,
holding a cactus wren in her thin brown hands.
They say if a river ever flowed here at the foot of the Peloncillos,
it's been dead for a century.
There's no use looking through old campaign maps, or
the torn diaries of cavalry officers, or the delicate letters
their wives sent back East, like pioneer tears
for fringe on those Tiffany lamps.
Because you will never resurrect a river
from the dust of a library,
and Cochise County is a cemetery of rivers.
There are days when I want to drink glass after glass of this sand.
I want to drink to the bottom of this mystery.
Down to all of the love, all of the death.
Down to the day the Mother of God reappears
in a flowing dress that is blue and green and sewn
with small gold threads.
It's ridiculous, and maybe it's wrong,
but when she lays down under the thighs of the young
cottonwood, the gold threads leap off.
They're river otters and cattails and trout.
And that's how she gives herself back to us.
Mine's a joy that makes no sense.

Victoria Edwards Tester is the winner of the Academy of American Poets Brazos Bookstore Prize and the Donald Barthelme Memorial Fellowship for Poetry. Her debut poetry collection, *Miracles of Sainted Earth*, received the WILLA Literary Award. She lives near Silver City, New Mexico.

Release

Rae Marie Taylor

> If we want to be happy at all, I think, we have to acknowledge that the
> circumstances which encourage us in our love of this existence are essential.
> —William Kittredge
> *A Hole in the Sky*

B etween the rain and a sudden hail shower, there is a quiet, pithy jubilance among us. The ribbon of run-off tumbles steadily down from the mountain towards the two small gates. We watch. The time has come. Down, past the trees, towards us, the water flows, soothing our cells. Reaching the shore where we stand, it branches under one already opened gate, flowing into the Santa Fe River, until the children's pulling and turning on the acequia's gate redirects its course. Was their delight any greater than our adult joy as we watched the children being shown how to open the gates under Phil's steady hand and buoyant flash of smile?

Release comes, the water trickling first, then splashing into the *acequia madre*, our acequia, spreading into a deep hole in the dry bed, gurgling, then free, moving now down toward the culvert, and through it, alive on its seven mile course. Good water. Beautiful ditch. We watch. Then play again as Phil opens the Santa Fe River gate wider for a moment to show the kids the rush of a falls. *Querencia!*

The same thrill of water had come to me years before in my studio on the Santa Fe River. Occasionally, while I was sculpting, a tumultuous rush of water would rise and pound outside the window during a thunderstorm. Energized, exhilarated, enveloped by the ozone, I would stand and take in the sight of the sudden rapids cascading by, in what was only moments ago a dry riverbed. The water was especially reassuring in those years, the 90s, as it was too often shut off at the reservoir above, and cans, wine bottles, other litter became as common as water might have been. It was a time when storing the run-off from the snow in the mountain reservoirs was considered good water management for an arid climate.

Sad vegetation, tattered eroding banks, lack of water itself, bulldozers flattening the shores, the all too common trash, are familiar to us in the Southwest, and are all signs of a habitat under duress. When we amble along beside a dying river, we are cut short, disheartened by the imbalance, the sometimes overwhelming physical sense of neglect. Naturally these realities undermine our courage and our connection.

Acequia Madre flowing between Osage Ave and Ashbaugh Park. © Julie West

There is a point, the naturalist Robert Finch asserts, in our relationship with a place when in spite of ourselves, we realize we do not care so much anymore, when we begin to be convinced, against our very wills, that our neighborhood, our town, or the land as a whole is already lost. The local landscape is no longer perceived as a "living breathing, beautiful counterpart to human existence," but something that has suffered irreversible brain death.

This is too often true. In so many places, we have brought about a place devoid of the moving holy. Our water, our very food, our spiritual sustenance depend on our restoring our affection for the land. As much as we live with the risk or the actual experience of disaffection from the land—and we do—we can still take heart in the places, traditions and symbols where we can restore both our affection and the earth. Precious as rivers have been over the centuries to the land itself and its animals and peoples, a living, flowing Santa Fe River, source of irrigation, of drinking water, of beauty, is our palpable heartline.

On a bright Friday afternoon, as the February snow melted and softened the clay earth outside, Dominique welcomed me into the warmth of her straw bale adobe home where I had come to hear more of her story. "Passionate, it was a *passion*, like a love relationship," she repeats with delight as she recounts her childlike rapport with the river and her enthusiasm each time she rode her bike to its shores, dedicated to its cleansing, curious as to what its offerings would bring that day. The river needed attention, the intention of her ritual.

Profoundly distressed at the sight of the trashed and sorry state of the Rio Grande on a visit to Taos in 1986, Dominique had been moved to make a pilgrimage of sorts. For seven years (from 1987 - 1994), on the 17th of every month, she walked the mostly dry bed of the Santa Fe River, a tributary of the Rio Grande, cleaning it and blessing it with ritual. An artist already committed to the spiritual in art at the time, she made this her artwork: a ritual performance, a witnessing, a healing.

She speaks of the first sadness of seeing the pollution, the neglect, and lack of life in the river bed itself and among the natural debris, its banks trashed with dildos, discarded furniture, soiled blankets, of course the myriad cigarette butts, and the needles reflecting the drug use along its dead shores. But the river offered gifts as well. A Jesus statue surfaced, and a copy of *Black Elk Speaks* "coincidentally" appeared out of the ruin on the day a Native American teacher had brought some students to join in the cleaning. "Magic, the river was magic," she repeats, enjoying still the significance of this synchronicity. One day a Hispanic man approached with "You want trash? I got trash," and offered to show her serious trash in his yard. This encounter led to cleaning first, of course, then to the planting of a community garden for him and his friends who happened to be part of the drug culture.

Magic too were the shoes, numerous shoes, starting with a little pair of Mary Jane's. Such an appropriate artifact for her story as she tells of the playfulness in the bending and bagging, the hopping and climbing among the banks enlivening within her a whole new childlike spirit.

Reading excerpts of Dominique's journal, I am reminded of Aboriginal songlines. "Partaking of the river's feast," she writes, "i am simply dancing the song of my heart." Suffering and exuberance, defeat and healing. In the Aboriginal songlines, like in the Inuit hunting songs, land and human echo each other, the songs mapping the trees and boulders, shelters, dunes, or ice floes guiding the people across known and unknown country. Dominique's monthly ritual created a new heart geography for her, for others. Her act, her *song* reminding us all: the water needs our care. Her ritual art wove the love of the river with those who occasionally joined her as she repeatedly did the necessary bending and bowing, an unusual kind of genuflection. Jay Griffiths, in her book, *Wild: An Elemental Journey,* quotes the Aboriginal painter and story-doctor, Margaret-Kemarre Turner, who knows the reciprocal power of place. "Going to a place keeps it alive," she says, "and keeps you alive too." This was happening here on Dominique's solitary walks. This we know — in our own heart, our own breath — as we too walk along. This happens as, our skin refreshed, our eyes rested, we meander with the current.

Dominique followed the dry river bed before water engineers established that 40% of water is often lost to evaporation in the reservoirs; before environmental science and practices in Australia and South Africa as well as Texas, Colorado, and Arizona renewed understanding of the importance in keeping the water moving for humans, the ground water, aquifers, the fish and the riparian habitat itself.

This artist walked years before our current Mayor committed to restoring the river by letting it run at regular intervals as a living entity; before he and ¡YouthWorks! in 2001 developed the Santa Fe Youth Corps, engaging youth from all backgrounds to help rid sections of the river of trash, uproot invasive species, design some conservation measures, and do some of the plain but intelligently designed hard, necessary work with boulders and rocks that naturally reinforce the river bed, slow down erosion from storm water run-off, and create elegant, healthy new meanders.

Dominique's pilgrimage ended in 1994, as more water entered the river and the work became lonely, even a little frightening, the further south of town she went. Thirteen years later, on Earth Day, the city convened the community at large to participate in planting fresh cottonwoods and willows along its banks. So many showed up. Men, women, and children energetically rolled up their sleeves, heartened by intergenerational efforts, soothed by the aliveness of the restored sections of the river. Days later, walking alone along the newly graceful shores of the river south of town, I joined many others in hoping for the continued flow of water.

Again this early spring of 2008, another friend relates the nimble joy of children scampering up and down the banks picking up the trash, and her own pride at how pristine her section of the river becomes. In our dry climate it is a keen pleasure knowing that the water about to come will seep in, not just under the river bed, but nourish the land and ground water up to hundreds of feet on either side. "Nurture the country because the country will always nurture you," Margaret Kamarre-Turner reminds us again.

Wholly engaged in healing the river—the humble, dirty, delightful process—Dominique's art ritual began with what she called the "matter" of "trickle trash, disrespect and despair." With repeated gestures of her ritual, "work as a garbologist," she says smiling, listening to the beauty of the river even without water, she brought it alive, healing herself as well, and along with her the people she encountered, all the while moving our culture toward repair and finer knowledge of the land. I can't help but see this pilgrimage as contributing to a kind of continuity in the river's life and the culture around it: a buildup toward a continuum with Dominique's solitary commitment to river care eventually engendering that of the city's—and the larger community's—care and concern.

The awareness of place gained in paying attention, touching and cleaning this narrow bed of earth goes beyond its immediate banks. "Standing in the riverbed, the vein of the earth!" Dominique exclaims, evoking for me the weaving through the land, not only of the Santa Fe river, but the Rio Grande too, and the

Colorado, on through their tributaries and up to their head waters. In the bright intensity of her dark eyes shines the visceral knowledge, an ancient knowledge of, "Our holy river...the whole American network of rivers. Soon...a diamond web stretching over the Earth."

Girl considers taking a second dip in this Santa Fe River swimming hole while her mother fishes upstream. Photograph by EC Ryan.

We are learning again this ancient knowledge that in the care of the river, we experience a physical, communal, and symbolic place where we can love the circumstances of our existence, reviving our affection for the land, putting it first over our habits as consumers and believers in pursuit and progress. Refurbishing our daily experience of beauty, nourishing our communal bonds and traditions, the vitality of a living Santa Fe River sustains our future.

∿

Spoken word poet Rae Marie Taylor's semi-nomadic life bridges her Southwest homeland and the Quebec North Country. In the City Different, she formerly coordinated conferences for Recursos de Santa Fe, including The Taos Conference on Writing and the Natural World and the Recursos Santa Fe Writers' Conference. Currently Taylor is completing a book of essays concerned with our beloved and beleaguered earth.

Flotsam Along the Rito Santa Fe

Paige Anna Grant

Early in the life of the Santa Fe Watershed Association, casting about for ways to reintroduce the town to its largely forgotten river, we started the Neighborhood River Watch project. Volunteers would visit a particular reach of the river once a month and record its condition; we would then compile a report from the checklists submitted by these volunteer stewards, and outrage the public with our expose of a dewatered, degraded, dumped-on little stream that had been the heart of Santa Fe since long before it acquired its Spanish name. We hoped that our muckraking would result in a wave of support to restore the river.

That wave was more of a trickle, but it has been a steadily growing trickle, and we learned a good deal from our River Watch. We mapped the culverts that daylighted at the river channel (the city had no record of them), and met with the Mayor and the City Engineer to point out the place in the heart of downtown where raw sewage leaked (and still leaks) steadily from a storm drain into the river. We learned that the derelict river sheltered people who had been discarded by society in much the same way that we had turned our backs on our little stream.

"Hi, whutchuguys doin?" He was nestled under a bridge, tucking into his first beer of the morning.

"We're trying to keep track of how the river's eroding and the dirty water that gets dumped into it."

"Oh, hey, that's a good thing. This little river needs some attention. Lots of people don't even know it's here. You know about the old Indian gardens along here? Yeah, they used to plant up on that bench. Lotta history down here. Well, God bless you guys."

Cars rushed past overhead, their drivers bent on their errands, oblivious to the world that was this cheerful man's home. Yet for all his affection for the place, he and his fellow bridge dwellers had little sense of responsibility to manage their impacts on the river they inhabited. They lived among, and eventually walked away from, the detritus of their lives, from bottles and cans and discarded sleeping bags to feces and the occasional syringe.

Despite the junk we had to step around, we Riverwatchers delighted in our monthly trips into the river channel, which took us to a secret garden a stone's throw from fancy restaurants and the halls of government. Here garter snakes darted from underfoot, butterflies blessed wildflowers, birds sat quietly on their nests, hoping you wouldn't notice, willows grew jungle-thick, and, yes, occasionally the stream flowed and brought with it all the enchantment that moving water creates in our animal minds. The flow would be storm runoff or a release from the dams upstream as the managers made room to store snowmelt in the spring. A flow of a few days was a thing to celebrate; a month-long spell of a living river made you believe in a better world.

Picking up trash on "Love Your River Day." Photograph by A. Kyce Bello.

Once, on a solo monitoring trip, parting the willows to find a path, I was surprised by a pair of Native American men moving upstream, an old man and a younger one, both with chin-length hair held back by cloth strips around their foreheads. They were equally surprised to see me. I explained my errand, and asked theirs. "We're going to look for Turtle Spring," the older man said. "My grandfather used to bring me down here to visit that place. It's been a long time I haven't been back."

"I'm down here a lot, and I don't know of any springs—just seeps in the riverbed here and there," I said. The old man shrugged and they moved on. Later, studying how the river had been dewatered, I learned that there used to be a spring-fed carp pond in the Bishop's Garden south of the cathedral. That spring was the source of a stream called the Rio Chiquito that flowed down what is now Water Street to join the Santa Fe River near the Santuario de Guadalupe. It was now buried under a parking lot. I wonder if that was Turtle Spring, and what it meant to the pueblo people that belonged to this landscape, and how many still remember it ought to be there and ought to be honored.

Carp pond in Archbishop's garden near Saint Francis Cathedral, circa 1887. Courtesy Palace of the Governors Photo Archive (NMHM/DCA). Negative No. 15264.

The Neighborhood River Watch morphed into the Adopt-the-River program, enlisting volunteers to steward a section of the river, clearing it of trash and helping to re-establish native vegetation. As with the monitoring project, the underlying objective was to create a constituency for the river: people who knew and loved it and would push politically for the city to include flow for the river in their water management plans. Another purpose of our visits was to demonstrate to the open-air community, as they sometimes called themselves, that the river belonged to all of us, and some of us thought it important to take care of our things....

It's a Saturday morning, and Sierra Club volunteers are picking up trash in the reach of the river they have taken on as stewards. The brown water is flecked with foam brewed from rags and leaves. A cell phone—flung from a snatched purse, perhaps—glints in willow shade. Styrofoam peanuts are drifted like hail. A CD and a saw blade shine in the undergrowth. A car seat is set up on the riverbank like Archie Bunker's lounger—home base for a homeless man. The stream gage is scribbled with angry tags. Whiskey bottles, tennis shoes, torn snapshots, sodden muddy towels—we put it all in black bags, and haul it to the curb for pickup by the City Parks Department. On the sidewalk is a mandala in colored chalk and the caption "You are light becoming life." We have been blessed.

"Should I clean up that junk over there?"

"No, that looks like somebody's camp. Go ahead and leave them a trash bag, though—sometimes they'll pick up after themselves if we leave them a bag to do it."

A weather-beaten blond woman in her thirties calls across the channel, "You guys doing community service?"

"Yes," I begin. My companion, a neighbor of the river who has come out this once to help, cuts me off. "No, we ain't, we're cleaning up the environment!" I had forgotten that most people picking up trash are working off a DWI rap.

"Hey, that's great! Can I have a bag? I'll pick up stuff on this side."

A volunteer passes a full bag up to me and clambers out of the channel. "There were three guys down there snoring away," she says. "I felt like knocking and saying, "Housekeeping! Would you like your sheets changed?"

The guardian angel of this section of the river, who has picked up trash and painted over graffiti along these blocks for most of a decade, says all the effort is paying off. He has found that if you slap paint over a tag as soon as it appears, the tagging subsides; if you keep the channel clean, it doesn't present the visual suggestion that, "It's OK, it's already trashed, it doesn't matter if I toss my can/bottle/bag of leftovers over the side." He thinks the regular presence of regular folks helps, too: the river is not such a refuge for unhealthy activities as it used to be. "I used to pick up a dozen needles every time I came out here. I hardly ever see one any more."

The steady trickle of effort to restore the Santa Fe River is building toward maintaining an ankle-deep stream for most of the year, paralleled by a trail for cyclists and pedestrians who will become river constituents and insist on protecting this green heart of Santa Fe. A trial "environmental flow" took place in September 2008. The understanding that a sustained small flow in the river contributes to recharge of municipal wells is beginning to gain currency. We can use our streamflow twice—once to keep the river alive and again for our drinking water supply.

There are sustained efforts as well to provide better options to the people who nest in the willows along the river. A newsletter from St. Elizabeth Emergency Shelter, located a few blocks offstream, told the story of Jimmy and John, brothers who had crisscrossed the country on foot, first for adventure and then in search of help for John's worsening schizophrenia. "[St. E's] taught us to look at ourselves for answers instead of sitting under a bridge with a beer waiting for a genie to come out of the bottle and save us," Jimmy said. The brothers were placed at

Casa Cerrillos, St. Elizabeth's transitional housing program for individuals with disabilities. With intensive counseling, John made progress on becoming less dependent on his brother as a caregiver. Jimmy stayed nearby, though: he became a resident manager at Casa Cerrillos with his own apartment, and helped clients move in and out while assisting with maintenance and repairs.

"We've done a lot of walking through the southern and western U.S. and seen some amazing things," Jimmy told the author of the newsletter. "But the drug and alcohol addiction was killing us and we had to stop. This program has given us the time and chance to decide what we wanted to do for the rest of our lives, and it's let me see that I could be a healthy person and a productive and participating part of society."

Jimmy and John have moved on—they were on their way to California, the last St. E's had heard. But they moved on wiser and steadier than when they came. As we are our brothers' keepers, we are our river's keepers. We have inherited this stream and its watershed from the pueblo people who planted squash on the river bench, the Spanish who diverted its water into acequias, the Yankees who built the dams. During our tenancy we have filled the landscape with streets and structures, pumped down the water table so the springs don't flow, imported water from farther and farther away to keep the town growing. The post-petroleum generations will have to figure out what to do with these wide, hot streets that shed water too quickly into fragile arroyos; how to grow their food closer to home; how to live within their means, surviving on and delighting in what the local landscape can provide, and protecting it for those who come after.

Daunting challenges. At least we can make sure they begin their turn at stewardship with a living river and a creed of kindness.

~~~

Paige Anna Grant is a hydrologist, storyteller, singer of old songs, and a Santa Fe resident for over a quarter century.

The Sweet Return

Jennifer Ferraro

There is in me
a place set free
by your momentum

And a quietude
seldom seen
that your surface calls out;

Sand-river, artifact of loss,
you mean comings and goings
and death ever-cleaved to life;

Just as the ruined wall
that stands in the green field
contains both possibility and grief

and the landscape is more beautiful for it—
We have been dry for so long
ghost river, just like you,
longing to have our gates flooded open,

to become sustenance, shade, refreshment;
In the ruined heart, they say
there is hope for a treasure—

And so I pray

May we be wet again,
may we overflow our banks
grown green and leafy;

May the fairies dance with us,
our words call forth hidden water and thunder
able to conjure and praise things into being;

Finally seeping down
beneath the earth of what is visible
to feed from the dark well-spring—

May we weep openly
for what is worth saving,
for what was almost lost,

for what is almost recovered:

for the sweet return
that is coming,
that is more beautiful

because of death.

✑

Poet and artist Jennifer Ferraro is the author/translator of *Quarreling with God: Mystic Rebel Poems of the Dervishes of Turkey*, and *Divine Nostalgia: Poems*. She has an MFA in Creative Writing from the University of New Mexico, and has created collaborative performances with other artists exploring beauty and the sacred feminine.

Fed by groundwater, some downtown sections of the river remain wet year round.
Photograph by EC Ryan.

Thinking River Thoughts

Caroline Fraser

> For myself I choose to listen to the river for a while, thinking river
> thoughts, before joining the night and the stars.
>
> — Edward Abbey
> *Desert Solitaire*

Sitting in traffic on Cerrillos Road, you might think you're miles from the nearest outdoor oasis, but have faith: You're only moments away from a conservation renaissance on the Santa Fe River. Yes, that Santa Fe River, for too many years a dry, dead ditch. Now, through the combined efforts of city and county officials, dedicated staff at the Santa Fe Watershed Association and WildEarth Guardians, and volunteers across the city, the River is coming back.

For over a decade, the Watershed Association has been lobbying to "re-water" the river. In 2007, they scored a public relations coup when our river, a tributary of the Rio Grande, was declared the most endangered in the country, part of a national campaign to focus attention on threats to natural watersheds. The publicity encouraged city officials to take a good hard look at the argument for putting water back where it belonged. It made business sense, with the potential for improving property values and attracting tourists to nearby cafes, restaurants, galleries, and walkways. Most important, restoring the ecological health of the entire riparian corridor would provide what Carol Norton, at WildEarth, calls "our best response" to the disquieting fact that "the southwest is Ground Zero for climate change." In a town where everyone keeps an anxious eye on the mountain snowpack, the importance of something we can't see — underground aquifers systematically starved for decades — has begun to seep in to the collective consciousness. Mayor Coss and the City Council took a major step in 2009, voting unanimously for a River Flow Resolution to restore water until at least the end of July. If there's enough in the reservoir, the flow may continue until September.

But water is only one part of the restoration equation. While old-timers remember a day when the riverbed through the center of town was only a few inches deep, it is now a deep chasm, carved by furious storm runoff funneled there by intensive development. Too-fast flows eroded the banks, carving a channel over twenty feet deep in some places. A recent bioengineering project helped stabilize the banks and slow the flow by restoring a more meandering course, but there's still work to be done. ¡YouthWorks! lent a hand by cleaning up debris, and now WildEarth is helping the river recover a cool green umbrella of native vegetation to further stabilize its battered banks, cool its water, and lure back an ark of life. In 2009, the Guardians and their volunteers planted 10,000 willows, 250 cottonwood, and a couple of hundred plants of "forage species"—food for birds and other native animals—including chokecherry, New Mexico golden currant, hackberry, and box elder maple. ¡YouthWorks! and WildEarth have also removed invasives, water hogs like salt cedar, Siberian elm, and Russian olive. The river is reaping the rewards—kingfishers are returning, along with Cooper's hawk, red-tailed hawk, owls, and long-tailed weasel—and so are we. As this corridor returns to health, it will reduce the urban heat island effect while offering opportunities for recreation, from anglers to toddlers.

On a recent visit to the Santa Fe River Preserve south of the water treatment plant, the river truly felt like an oasis, lush, cool, and calm. Willows and cottonwoods were flourishing. Cattails grew high in marshy spots, and red-winged blackbirds called. Ducks flew overhead, and swallows swooped by, scooping insects out of the air. Jim Matison, WildEarth's restoration program director, says that Rio Grande chub are returning, and dace as well. Miles upriver, in the Nature Conservancy's Santa Fe Canyon Preserve, beavers have set up shop, building dams and lodges. Their activities, too, are essential to river restoration, impounding water, helping to deepen and recharge aquifers, and providing rich habitat for scores of other creatures.

But the river renaissance is not only taking place on the outskirts of town. New cottonwoods and willows, just leafing out, grace the riverbanks along West Alameda, in the Bicentennial Park. And the Santa Fe River Trail—the perfect way to bring Santa Feans back in touch with the natural heart of the community—is finally coming to fruition. Long a dream of bikers, trail runners, and dog walkers, the trail was first envisioned decades ago but stalled for years while the city struggled to put the pieces in place, winning $1.4 million in bond funding and negotiating easements with property owners. Once finished, the trail will stretch from Patrick Smith Park near the top of Canyon Road to N.M. 599, and may eventually be extended south to the wastewater treatment plant.

From a dead ditch to a living river: Restoring this historic watershed, from its headwaters in the Sangre de Cristos to its passage through the city, is creating jobs, improving water quality, revitalizing the landscape, and literally forging connections between Santa Fe and the greater ecosystem that surrounds it. Thinking river thoughts—and acting on them—is the ultimate in sustainability.

~~~

Caroline Fraser is the author of *Rewilding the World: Dispatches from the Conservation Revolution.* A journalist whose work has appeared in *The New Yorker*, *The Atlantic Monthly*, and *Outside Magazine*, Fraser traveled to six continents to report on large-scale conservation and restoration projects.

Local River, Local Food

Pat D'Andrea

*I*magine that water in the Santa Fe River could grow food. Putting water back into the river could give us orchards and vegetable gardens. Imagine that hometown kids become gardeners.

When Pedro de Peralta and his troops arrived in Santa Fe in 1609 they carried city planning instructions written in 1573 by King Phillip II of Spain. The instructions called for forest reserves, openness to the cleansing north winds, and access to fresh flowing water. Just where native people had established homes and fields long before, the conquistadores put down their roots. It took the river to anchor the city and provide food for its people.

But ideas about what the river was for had changed profoundly by the 1800s. The river became the source for year-round plumbing. The dams at McClure and Nichols dried up the gardens below headwaters, flash floods from the big arroyos that fed the river helped deepen the river channel, the springs that used to feed its flows diminished.

Nowadays, we want a flowing river at the heart of our town. In the upper reaches, where the water flows most often, there are green parks, old trees, places for visitors to sit and dogs to run, spots where kids can explore. Beyond St. Francis Drive the river changes and where gardens used to be there are none. The river needs flowing water in these reaches. The river needs to live.

I think we may be in danger of wanting something — water flowing in the river — that is only an "artifact" in a town that caters to visitors. Desert rivers are often dry on the surface, running only when the rains or spring runoff comes. River water is good for the soul, as we all know, but I wonder whether an always-flowing Santa Fe River would be just another decoration.

Thirty years ago, in *The Death of Nature*, Bill McKibben warned of the danger posed by increasing levels of greenhouse gases in the atmosphere. It took twenty years before the idea of global climate change, or warming, became a household concern. In the past few years we have begun to feel the effects of climate change. It is wet when we expect dry, dry when we think it used to be wet, trees are dying from bark beetle infestations stoked by a drought, and the summers are hotter than ever.

The city's food supply, much of which still comes from far away, is getting more costly and uncertain. We know more about how foods have to be treated with chemicals to withstand long travel times, and supermarket shelves are sometimes empty when we've always expected them to be full. Local food supplies are becoming more important and more valuable.

In the memory of some people in Agua Fria village there is a connection between the Santa Fe River and the Rio Grande. The Santa Fe River flowed to the Rio Grande, and on the way it watered fields; that's what some people remember.

Our river still goes to the Rio Grande, because there's a sewage treatment on its bank. The plant cleans up used water from the city and pours it back into the riverbed. Below the plant's outfall there are bosques and flourishing bankside plants watered by the perennial flow.

Upstream, from Camino Alire downstream to the treatment plant, the riverbed is most often dry, deeply incised by flash floods, with crumbling banks and little stabilizing vegetation. That reach of the river is where the Spanish and native farms used to be.

What is the river for? I think it's for growing things. I think the reason for water in the river should be more than what salves our souls, as important as that may be. I think the river can, could and should help to feed us now as it did before. This is a time when we need more than the romance of flowing water to keep ourselves whole. It's time to add practicality to the romance.

~~~

Pat D'Andrea grew up in New Mexico, drank straight from the Rio Grande when she was a kid, and wants to eat peaches watered by the Santa Fe River.

Log footbridge and headgate on Acequia Madre, Santa Fe. Date unknown. Bergere Family
Photograph Collection. Courtesy New Mexico State Records Center and Archives. Image
No. 23426.

El Agua de Mi Abuelo

Pilar F. Trujillo

Most days during the balmy, summer months I wake up to the sound of the acequia running right outside my bedroom window. This is the time of year when the snow has already melted from Truchas peak and surely as ever made its way down the Rio Quemado all the way to our Acequia de la Cañada Ancha in Chimayó. I wake up tired because it's early and the majority of the work on our fields needs to be done before noon, before the hottest part of the day. I grumble about this business of waking up so early to my brothers, but in secret I like it. It's peaceful. On any given day and depending on the time of year, there is more than enough work to go around the farm. The fields need to be cleared and prepared, or the seeds need to be cleaned, or the headgate controlling the flow of water needs to be fixed, or the *surcos* (rows) need to be made or fixed, or it's time to plant, or it's time to harvest, or it's time to irrigate, or it's time to make *ristras*, or roast the chile, and of course there are always weeds and more weeds to be pulled. Time is not linear in any sense on a farm, and neither is the work. We are just beginning to learn the cycles of our land, adjusting our bodies and hearts. This practice is not special or unique to my family here in northern New Mexico. To be sure you could say that this work is in the blood of all people, but more immediately, it is in the blood of every *norteño* and every native person, passed onto us by our ancestors. The land is our body, the work is in our blood, the acequia is our heart pumping blood and giving life to our body. This is how we were born.

When I think about waterways or about the Santa Fe River, I think about the people that used to know the river like I have gotten to know the acequia outside my window. There are probably people that still remember. I have met people like them. People like Louie from Tesuque, who knows the original Tewa names of the mountains and watershed that feed the Santa Fe River, who knows the old ways of using the land as a sponge. I think of people like Victor from Questa, who makes his living from his farm that is 7500 feet in elevation and only a few miles south of the Colorado border. Victor cries when he talks about water because he knows that he is talking about God, about that which sustains his way of life. I think of all the people who understand the tricks of properly irrigating with an acequia, how to be intimate with the water and get it to go where you want it, those who truly know that irrigating this way is an art form. I think about the *bendiciones* (blessings) that are said at the beginning of every season, out in the fields and over the acequias, honoring the sacredness of the water and the land.

When I think about the Santa Fe River, I think about my grandfather Cipriano Trujillo of Chimayó, whose land we inherited and plant today. My grandfather, whose upbringing was so hard that he couldn't imagine tending the fields willingly and without the need for survival, did not pass his knowledge directly to us. The intimacy he had with the land and the water is something that my brothers and I have had to relearn after years of living and working in the city, of pot smoking, partying, and buying our food from stores. After years of disconnect, we seek to find ourselves again, my brothers and I. We find ourselves living in Chimayó. And together we are working the farm. At first we take advice from anybody who's willing to dispense it. There are a lot of people who have an idea of what farming is about. We hire a nice boy from Vermont, Daniel, who lives with us and has an extended knowledge of organic farming—in Vermont. He struggles with the challenge of growing food at 6500 feet with little water, and we struggle with conveying to him the things about farming that we seem to inherently know. Daniel has a hard time believing us when we tell him that the native chile doesn't need to be irrigated every day. He thinks it's dying or suffering, but we know, somehow, that it loves the heat, loves the challenge of surviving and thriving in this climate. We are proud of ourselves, looking at our calloused hands at the end of the day, acknowledging the information that we are regaining. I like the idea that our hands are able to remember the work.

Can you imagine what it would mean for the city of Santa Fe to regain this information as well? If you ask the right people, I'm sure you can still hear the stories around the Santa Fe River, learn the same lessons I'm learning in Chimayó. Can you imagine having a living river that feeds dozens of acequias, instead of just a handful of *parciantes* (acequia irrigators) on the Acequia Madre? If you drive down Agua Fria or West Alameda, the fields are still there, quietly waiting. They hold horses now, or a mobile home here and there, but can you imagine instead you see gorgeous irrigated fields of alfalfa or corn or chile? You see youth learning how to flood irrigate with their neighbor or grandpa. You see beautiful, large cottonwoods dotting the riverbank and owls, hawks and squirrels all making their homes in the trees. You see families and neighbors helping each other with planting or harvesting. You see chile *ristras* hanging outside of porches not for decoration, but because the people grew that chile and are intending to eat it once it dries. You see children running happily through the *bosque*, finding frogs and salamanders and getting their feet wet in the soggy riverbed. You see a community coming together, planting, weeding, harvesting.

This traditional knowledge is not completely lost, but rather displaced by sidewalks and pavement, businesses and bigger homes. But it is still there; we still have a chance to bring it back. Imagine waking up most days to the sound of water running right outside your window.

~cc

Pilar F. Trujillo was born and raised in Española. She now lives in Chimayó where she is helping her family grow chile and other vegetables on their ancestral farmland. She has a degree in Environmental Studies from Prescott College and works as the Youth Coordinator for the New Mexico Acequia Association, where she encourages local youth to grow food that is spiritually and culturally meaningful to their traditional communities.

Fleeting summer flow. Photograph by EC Ryan.

River Reeds of Golden Dawn

Gregory Gutin

Who will catch me as I fall
From this ledge of golden grass
Where fields of hanging chili and rows
Of speckled corn sprouted forth so tall?
From this slope
Upon which the daughters of horse-thieves
And sons of half-native mothers
Were born in shrunken mud and clay homes?
From here the mountains cast
An evening blood-light across this gradual valley
Into the eyes of the once holy child of faith,
Now our oldest, greatest grandfather.

Overgrown now
By widened roads and thirsty strangers,
It was here that the silver milk from Her
Pine and spruce laden breasts
Came pouring forth, seeping
Down the crooked valley
Of birdsongs, elk calls
And coyotes chasing river hawks
Back towards the sky.

Can you hear their distant calls,
Cries like the dry wind of yesterday's storm?
They wait beside a crumbling bank
Of brittle branches and leaves
Eyes closed and dreaming,
For the water has ceased to flow in this Mother's heart—
Its wet reflection of yesterday's storm
Speaks only in riddles today.

They look back at us, silently, the unseen ones,
As we dig still deeper to discover ourselves

In the shells and shards
Left here by long forgotten history.
Could we remember that melody,
That song of precious nectar,
The seeds of twisted trees whose leaves
Are blowing dry now in the modern wind of our village?

I will stomp and dance and pray
To the sleeping spirits of this broken Mother's land—
She must be quite hungry, and rightly so!
She has waited there, patiently, beside slow granite stones
With her hands reaching out
For the gift of my freshly-woven woolen belt.
Hidden within its deep ochre design
Lives a swimming river of azure beauty
Meandering like a snake, a root, or a tear
Down the cheek of the faceless deity,
She who will swallow it whole as a long overdue offering.

Though it is only a single drop of dew
In this hottest of summer suns,
She is drinking again.
The ground trembles, thanking us
For remembering her deepest desire to flow,
Alive and living still,
But unable yet to move as she once knew how.

Walk with me the entire way
To this canyon cut deep by her grief.
It is also our own,
And awaits us downstream, unavoidably.
If we only stand and watch
There will be no memory left,
No stories for our children to tell.
We will have only our tears to moisten
This high desert pool of patience and grace,
A collective mirror, shattered
Beneath the tired feet that carried us here.

Catch me, so we can sing
The water back to her home.
There will be no stopping this time
Of our ancestors' rushing return,

As wing-ed fish and river reeds of golden dawn
Come cracking forth through the crust of failing veils.
Catch me so we can swim again
In these dark, delicious waters of the holy soul,
Here where first we learned her song.

Gregory Gutin has lived as an artist, musician, and educator in New Mexico since 1992. He is committed to bringing awareness to the creative process as a way of life.

Bosque below the confluence of the Santa Fe River and Arroyo Torreón. Photograph by EC Ryan.

Restoring the River:
Research Shows Sustaining Steady Flows Might Be Easier Than Previously Thought
Staci Matlock
The Santa Fe New Mexican
May 30th 2008

This article explores how changes in managing releases of water from the reservoirs could provide water to the river for far longer than current practices allow. The amount of water that surges through the river during an average spring could, if released in a way that mimics the river's natural flow pattern, keep the river alive through the summer and fall while still maintaining sufficient supplies for the city.

~cc~

Engineer Neil Williams and The Nature Conservancy's Robert M. Findling paddled to the middle of Two Mile Pond in the Santa Fe River Preserve on a morning this week as the sun rose above the canyon. Around their canoe, swallows swooped above the water as red-winged black birds perched on thick stands of willow.

The men measured the pond's depth at several spots and found 7 feet was the deepest point. In the late 1800s, this pond was the main reservoir for Santa Fe's water. Upstream the water trickled between cottonwoods through the original Santa Fe River channel. It's a rare occurrence for this stretch of the river below the city's Nichols Reservoir, ever since the city built a bypass channel and rerouted occasional water releases around the pond.

Findling, Williams, Williams' co-researcher and wife, Paige Grant, Santa Fe Mayor David Coss and others want to see a more regular water flow restored in this stretch of the river's original channel and further downstream. Grant, a hydrologist, said the research she and Williams have conducted indicate keeping water in the river could be easier than people think.

She said they've gathered data on water flows into and out of the city's two current reservoirs — Nichols and McClure — for the past seven years. They found the city has released an average of 775 acre feet of water a year from Nichols, not counting the unusually wet year of 2005. The average includes 2002, a historic drought year for the river.

The Santa Fe Watershed Association, which paid for the water-flow study, is advocating the city dedicate 1,000 acre-feet of water a year to the river for an "environmental flow." (One acre-foot equals 325,851 gallons.) The city could reach the goal, "and it isn't even going to be painful," Grant said.

According to a recent proposal by Grant and Williams for restoring the river stretch from Nichols Reservoir to the Two Mile Pond, "A program of calibrated, year-round small releases could distribute these flows on a schedule that is better for fish habitat, aquifer recharge and riparian health. No additional water rights are needed to manage the release of these flows."

Right now any water in this stretch seeps from under the upper Nichols Reservoir and flows down from some side creeks. It's not coming from the millions of gallons of water a day currently being released from Nichols by the city's water division. Water flowing into Nichols and McClure has bumped levels up to 86 percent of capacity, and the real snowmelt flow in the mountains has just begun.

In 1994, the little Two Mile Reservoir was decommissioned and breached for safety reasons. Public Service Company of New Mexico later donated the property to The Nature Conservancy, which is working to restore wildlife habitat. The reservoir filled with sediment and became a pond.

Williams and Grant were at Two Mile Pond in The Nature Conservancy's Santa Fe River Preserve working on another research project Wednesday morning. They left floating probes in the reservoir that will read the water temperature every half hour and store the information for the couple to upload to computer later. They'll be checking the data through the summer to see if the temperatures remain cool enough to support populations of endangered fish like the Rio Grande chub. A small regular water flow into the pond would be important for a fish refuge, Grant said.

The research Grant, Williams and many other scientists have conducted over the years on water flow, quality, temperature and surrounding soils provide the scientific information that city officials and staff can use to decide how best to manage the watershed that feeds the Santa Fe River.

The Santa Fe Watershed Association is working to convince city officials that a new management scheme could provide water both for Santa Fe's needs and those of the river.

Near Two Mile Pond, giant trees lay crisscrossed on the ground, felled by beavers. A string of beaver dams stretched from the old dam at Two Mile Pond up to an even older stone dam.

Grant said the tree-gnawed evidence of beavers now extends down to Sandoval Street. She calls it a good sign. "I see it as a vote of confidence by the beavers that this river is going to come back," she said.

Investing in the Santa Fe River

David Groenfeldt

*W*ater is like money; it needs to circulate, to flow. Stagnant water loses its vibrancy, becomes polluted, and breeds disease. Flowing water is cleansing, purifying, liberating. There is a message here: Our Santa Fe River needs to flow. It needs to be itself. And just like money that circulates through a community, from the grocer to the plumber to taxes and to schools, bringing more benefits as it moves, so too our river needs to flow in order to bring us the many benefits that it has to offer.

In 2007, the Santa Fe River was designated the most endangered river in America by American Rivers, a national river advocacy group. Our river was awarded this distinction because of our local custom of impounding 100% of its water in our city reservoirs, leaving no water at all for the river itself. On the eve of our 400th anniversary, we have become the nation's poster child for unsustainable water management.

Since the 1940s there have been periodic calls to keep the river flowing year-round. But our citizens became accustomed to seeing the river go dry and accepted the conventional wisdom that storing all the water in the reservoirs was the only sensible way to manage a river in a dry climate. Meanwhile, the rest of the world began to recognize the long-term benefits of healthy rivers, *particularly* in dry climates like ours. The arid countries of Australia and South Africa adopted laws in the 1990s mandating that an environmental flow be maintained in their fragile rivers. The European Union followed their example in their new water law of 2001. Here in America, most of our neighboring states, including Texas, Colorado, and Arizona have taken steps to protect a minimum flow in their rivers.

But New Mexico has remained virtually silent on the issue of protecting riparian health, other than for meeting the nationally mandated Endangered Species Act. Fortunately, the city of Santa Fe has the flexibility to set its own water policies, since we have legal rights to most of the water in the Santa Fe River. We, the City Different, can choose a different, more sustainable path.

From Hoarding to Investing

Instead of hoarding the water in our reservoirs, we can *invest* that water in a way that will do the most good for the most people (and nature) for the longest time. Our current "hoarding" strategy calls for turning off the river and storing as much water as possible in the reservoirs. We use that water until it is depleted, which gives us about 40% of our total city water needs. Then we pump water from our local aquifers for another 20% and groundwater from the Buckman area for the remaining 40%. These Buckman wells are being over-drawn and are slated to be replaced by the Buckman Direct Diversion, which will take water out of the Rio Grande. Not included in this picture are more than 1,000 private wells within the city that are effectively unregulated, and the water they pump is unreported.

By investing a small flow of water from our reservoirs, instead of hoarding every drop, we could start repaying our debt to our groundwater, while at the same time providing a flowing river for our community. With a bit of water, our river would benefit not only us, the people of Santa Fe, but also the nature of Santa Fe — the trees and shrubs along the river that provides habitat for wildlife, and the water that provides habitat for insects and fish.

Downtown rockwork. Photograph by A. Kyce Bello.

How Much Water Does the River Need?

A release of 1,000 acre-feet of water per year (10% of total water use) would support a small continuous flow of slightly less than 1.5 cubic feet per second (cfs). How much water is that? Imagine a long line of 10 gallon fish tanks end-to-end; now remove the glass partitions, and that would be roughly the amount we're talking about. Most of that 1,000 acre-feet would infiltrate through the riverbed and into the aquifer. Estimates vary as to how much could be recovered from shallow wells, but the best use for the infiltrated water would not be immediate pumping, but long-term aquifer recharge to prepare for the next big drought. In other words, the best use of water flowing in the river is to store it in (or more accurately, to allow it to infiltrate into) the aquifer until we really need it to get through a serious drought. In the short term, that water would be repaying the debt to our aquifer that has been accumulating for the past several decades. But would we have enough water for our community if we let some of it flow down the river?

Where Could the "Extra" Water Come From?

If we are going to let water out of our reservoirs and into the river, we will have to get by with less water (through conservation) or find new water sources, for example, through systematic harvesting of rainwater from our roofs and other impermeable surfaces. Some steps could be implemented immediately, while other steps will take some planning and investment.

1. *Conservation.* We can easily save 10% more water—the equivalent of the flow we need for our river—through affordable conservation measures that do not noticeably affect our quality of life. One way is through technology: replacing sprinklers with drip irrigation; installing low-flow showerheads, and investing in low-water consuming clothes washers and dishwashers. But the easiest way to save water is also the most effective: simply use less of it. Turn the water on more slowly, and off more quickly, re-use the dishwater for the plants, take quick showers, etc. With a flowing river as our incentive, most Santa Feans would happily use less water and the aggregate effect could be huge. In Brisbane, Australia, a massive awareness campaign to save water cut per capita water use in half in just two weeks, and the city avoided running out of water. A "Save the Santa Fe River" campaign might have a similar impact.

2. *Rainwater Harvesting* for landscape irrigation. When the drip irrigation lines are connected not to the city water pipes but hooked up to water tanks storing rainwater from the roof, that is when we are on our way to a sustainable future. With the combination of roof catchment and drip irrigation, we could cut our summer landscape irrigation demand in half, saving between 1,000 and 1,500 acre feet of water, more than enough for a living river from this source alone.

3. *Stormwater Management.* When it rains in Santa Fe, water rushes off roofs, parking lots, and streets to arroyos and then to the river. Rather than viewing stormwater as a problem that erodes and pollutes, let's think of it as a resource that infiltrates and recharges our groundwater and revives the

springs that once fed our river. By integrating stormwater management with landscaping, much of the city's greenery could be irrigated from stormwater rather than city water, with the excess stormwater flows going into the groundwater and/or slowly seeping into the river. This approach takes planning, investment, but most importantly, a commitment to make use of this potentially valuable water resource.

4. *Wastewater Management.* Santa Fe is just beginning to tap into our wastewater as an important resource. We re-use about 1,000 acre-feet of water per year (for golf courses, parks, and playing fields) but with a total water budget of 10,000 acre-feet, we can do better. Some of the water now emitted from our centralized Wastewater Treatment Plant could be injected into the aquifer for later recovery as part of our drinking supply (it gets cleaned up along the way). The principle of using wastewater for aquifer recharge would be more practical with small, decentralized neighborhood facilities that could discharge locally into the river. The treated discharge would mix with the natural flow, maintaining adequate water quality and augmenting the quantity.

5. *Managing Reservoir Releases.* Nearly every spring, the city's two reservoirs fill from snowmelt, and water is released into the river. Past policies aimed at ensuring full reservoirs, so releases would not be authorized until it could be determined with 100% certainty that the melting snow pack would fill the reservoirs. This operating rule resulted in uncontrolled spills and very high volume releases causing channel and bank erosion. On average since 2001, some 700 acre-feet of water have been released each year, just to keep the reservoirs from spilling. Rather than releasing this water as an emergency overflow measure, this water could be released slowly throughout the year, while mimicking the natural flow pattern of the river: more flow during the spring run-off and the summer monsoon, less flow during the winter. Reservoir releases could also be managed in response to precipitation, to stretch the water even further, reducing releases during dry conditions, and increasing when conditions relax.

Conclusion

In a wet year, releasing water on a regular basis will free up reservoir space that will be filled by rain and melting snow, effectively increasing the flood storage capacity of the city without any new construction. In a dry year, releases of water into the river could be curtailed or even stopped. Our consolation would be that the water that was released and infiltrated has provided valuable services, both to the aquifer, and to the river corridor ecosystem: the trees and shrubs and the wildlife inhabiting or passing through.

Monsoon floodwater. Photograph by EC Ryan.

Reforming our policies requires a shift in the way we as a community conceptualize our river, our watershed, and our use of water. The Santa Fe River died — was sacrificed — because we assumed there was no other way of meeting our water needs. Australia has faced one of its worst droughts in history, yet their laws protecting the environmental status of rivers (even ephemeral streams) have remained in force, mandating that at least pulses of water be delivered to safeguard plants and aquatic life. When the drought is over, the streams can bounce back quickly because they are still alive; the full complement of aquatic life in those streams will be able to withstand the long drought thanks to water policies that recognize, by law, the intertwined destinies of people and Nature. We need a similar understanding of our co-dependence with Nature, and similar policies to safeguard the long-term health of our Santa Fe River.

~~~

An anthropologist by training, David Groenfeldt started his professional involvement with water by studying village irrigation in India as a graduate student. He has worked with the International Water Management Institute (IWMI) in Sri Lanka, with consulting firms on water and agriculture projects, and with the World Bank's water division. Groenfeldt served as Director of the Santa Fe Watershed Association from 2006 – 2009.

Bringing Our River Back to Life

Richard Schrader

Envisioning a restored Santa Fe River requires a leap of the imagination and, perhaps, a little faith and conviction. What is possible for the Santa Fe River depends on how we envision the river's potential as we begin to act collectively to enhance wild areas in the midst of our urban lives. How much are we ready to re-inhabit the floodplain, slow down our stormwater and direct it to open spaces and community gardens, and lead our families outside to reconnect with local parks? Let's take a walk down the Santa Fe River to see the land health problems at several areas in the watershed and envision how they might look if they were restored.

Slowing Water and Sediment in Upland Arroyos

Many of our arroyos are unstable with deep incised canyons that rarely let the water spread. Some of the headlands of these small watersheds have a fairly dense number of piñon or juniper trees, more than when fire occurred more frequently in the unpopulated hills. The typical pattern inside the city is to treat arroyos like storm drains in lieu of making land available to detain and slow down the first flood pulses. As a result many arroyos in the city look like someone took a powerful two-foot diameter pressure hose and started shearing off the banks and bottom of the channel. In other arroyos the channel's are widening and full of fresh sediment from eroding reaches upstream. Every couple of years homeless people die during big flood events in Santa Fe arroyos/storm drains, and erosion in the river worsens.

I envision holding water much longer in this watershed by rebuilding the soils and sponge capacity in arroyo banks. We can carefully thin some of the juniper to prevent "mounding" that comes from accelerated erosion around the base of these trees, and cut some of the branches and stems into posts to use as building material for erosion and water management structures. We can use rocks to create one-rock dams at key slopes in the hills to slow but not stop water flow, spreading it in thin sheets to settle out floating sediment. Rocks can also be used to hold bed elevations to slow or even reverse the down cutting that can happen in arroyo bottoms exposed to rushes of runoff from streets, buildings, and yards. In the future we will see more ponderosa pine, naturalized fruit trees such as apricot, or nitrogen-fixing New Mexico locust in these upland hills and arroyos.

Rewetting and Re-inhabiting Floodplain Terraces

Long ago the river frequently flooded a much wider area than gets flooded now. Beavers built dams using the abundant willow, cottonwoods, and even aspen that grew in banks and oxbows. I'm not exactly sure when large-scale down cutting started from St. Francis for several long reaches all the way past Lopez Lane Many sources point to the 1950s when a severe nine-year drought occurred, with the down cutting continuing to this day. The floodplain terraces were abandoned when many of the acequias and farms were developed because the land became more valuable for building than farming. City policies and studies in the 1970s show clear evidence of intent to make the river floodplain get deeper at the Alire Bridge—a photograph of a man holding a measuring rod near the entrance to La Conquistadora shows a potential flood that will inundate the subdivision unless the river bottom was excavated and lowered to prevent such a disaster.

The floodplain terrace at Frenchy's Field used to be wetted nearly every spring and summer with irrigation water from the Acequia de los Pinos and the *desague*/outflow of the Acequia Madre. An aerial photograph from 1951 shows a cottonwood bosque along the bank. Now the floodplain terrace is abandoned to the dry winds of spring and the recreational use of walkers, dogs, and all terrain vehicle use. The City is making efforts to create a community garden and ¡YouthWorks! began to address rampaging headcuts in the Arroyo de las Cruces next to the park formed by street runoff coming from Agua Fria, the park's parking lot, and urban development.

I see the possibility of harvesting huge amounts of water in the old acequia systems that worked for many years to wet Frenchy's Field but are now mostly used to rush water through and away from the park. The restored arroyos will refresh the shallow aquifers that help sustain the park's trees. A future community garden could include plants that tap into the refreshed groundwater that comes from the storm water and our streets and roofs. The garden will also become a gathering place for neighbors to plant and grow food, sharing food-generating strategies, and harvest the collective knowledge gained only from a group of people practicing the art of stewardship and restoration. In some places the terraces may be lowered next to the river to enable overbank flooding, oxbow/side channel development, and lush stands of cottonwood and willow to return to the banks of the river and arroyos at Frenchy's Field.

River Channel Returned to the River

The current stability and ecological function of the Santa Fe River channel is very poor as a result of several decades of lack of care and investment. I have seen trash ranging from large slabs of concrete, bed mattresses, and wheelbarrows flip, crash, and flood with tons of sediment down the channel during big storms. I have seen more than three-dozen vehicles racing and tearing through the river during summer thunderstorms or during spring snowmelt. In some places we have sewer pipes carrying our waste under the river bottom only a few feet from where trucks, cars, and motorcycles regularly cross the river. Banks of the Santa Fe River crumble under such pressure and the bottom of the stream becomes littered with erratic, large chunks of waste products that in turn make stormwater tear at its sandy bottom and aquifers and rip at its banks to get more space to spread.

Slowing the river with handmade check dams. Photograph by EC Ryan.

The old river crossing at Camino Carlos Rael is our city's poster-child for managing the river channel in the *wrong* way and the river conditions there mirror a lack of care and coordination. A large sewer pipe resists being torn out despite the traffic due to a tenuously anchored cement sill, which is held up on top of gabions (rock-filled baskets) that are falling apart. Efforts to plant trees and stabilize banks will never be successful until our local governments coordinate to make more space for a river than a very limiting width of 45 feet.

We need to work with the city and county to keep cars from tearing up riverbanks and racing through its river bottoms. The random couch, old bags of cement, and tumbling car parts need to be removed from the river as soon as they appear to prevent erratic erosion when floodwater hit the objects and carves at the banks or stream bottom. But even more important, restoring the river requires us to make more space for a wider floodplain that may have one channel and accessible terraces and side channels when it floods. We will also need carefully installed rock structures that encourage the river to meander, create pools where water is present longer, and hold or rebuild a veneer of soil to hold water like a sponge. In the several places where we have fragile and important infrastructure such as sewer main pipes or legally located domestic homes we must maintain the river bottom elevation and allow water to cascade through narrow areas using carefully constructed crossvanes. Between, underneath, and around the rock structures we will plant countless amounts of native wood species such as coyote willow, Rio Grande and narrowleaf cottonwood, and Gooding's black willow. Underneath the canopy of the newly established trees we hope to see running water coming for longer times and, particularly, at the right time. Our native plants need water when it would come naturally, with spring snowmelt and summer low-flows being some of the most critical times.

And, of course, our river needs water, at first in any amount that is possible! The city needs formalized commitments to a flowing Santa Fe River. We hope to have an assessment completed in 2009 on how much water needs to flow, when, and how long so that basic ecological values and functions are met in the river corridor. Then we and our government representatives need to take a courageous step of dedicating enough water to the river to bring it back to life.

What is the potential of a restored Santa Fe River? We have never been closer to seeing real change on the ground yet much of the needed work is yet to be done. We need to take actions in our daily lives to envision and realize through work restoration on our own particular reach. And we need to connect with other stewards upstream and downstream to share results and discuss what can do collectively to realize the potential of a river and community restored.

Richard Schrader started River Source in 1997 to develop projects with significant public involvement that lead to long-term and community-based landscape stewardship. River Source has designed restoration projects and set up ecological monitoring systems with private and public landowners on over 45 sites throughout New Mexico, including the Santa Fe and Galisteo watersheds.

The river in midsummer, just days before its flow is cut off. Photograph by EC Ryan.

An Ecologist's Perspective

Gerald Z. Jacobi

I have been fortunate in my life and professional career to have spent most of my time observing and investigating freshwater ecosystems such as rivers, lakes, and ponds. My interest has not diminished since my curiosity as a child first took me to the banks of a living river in a small town along the front range of Colorado over 60 years ago. Moving water dominated my time. I raced toy boats, trying to avoid back currents and large rocks which might slow the downstream drift. I spent hours lying on the banks looking into the water at aquatic insects as they moved their gills while trying to maintain position against the current. Several times I collected them in jars to take home to observe, later getting up during the night to see if they were still alive (they weren't), only to conclude they needed flowing water to survive (not knowing about respiration at the time). Fishing next caught my fancy, not only the thrill of catching an unknown, but to see what fish were eating. I examined stomach contents only to realize that insects and other invertebrates were important components in the diet of fish. I then tried to catch fish with artificial flies that I tied to imitate the immature and adult stages of insects, finally ascertaining that these two life stages were interconnected.

This early exposure to the aquatic natural world eventually led me to university teaching and research where I extolled the attributes of aquatic systems and the need for healthy rivers and watersheds in our lives. I exposed students to environmental ethics and encouraged them to pursue careers in environmental science. My professional career continues as a research biologist investigating the interconnectedness of the physical, chemical, and biological processes of freshwater ecosystems. I still look at flowing waters with wonder knowing they are extremely complex systems but can be enjoyed and appreciated without involving the details.

A living river is one which has an environmental flow satisfying all aspects of the riparian and instream biological community and is a constant reminder of the health of the watershed because activities upstream are manifest downstream. It contains a flow that provides water through time and space by mimicking the natural flow (hydrograph) and reflects the physical, chemical and biological integrity of the region. A river such as the Santa Fe River during pre-dam time may have been perennial some years and ephemeral others (with interrupted surface flow), but probably had reaches connected through sub-surface flow. Continuous perennial surface flows connected to the Rio Grande allowed native Rio Grande cutthroat trout and other fish to colonize upper reaches.

Presently in the high desert landscape of the southern Sangre de Cristo Mountains, rivers that reach the Rio Grande are few due to the vagaries in the weather and the multiple demands of humans on the water supply. In small free-flowing reaches such as the upper Santa Fe River, the natural water year begins with high spring flushing flows due to the melting of snow that accumulated during the winter. This increased flow wets the edge of the stream, flooding riparian vegetation like cottonwoods, willows, and grasses, and providing water that infiltrates and is stored in the flood plain for eventual slow release back into the channel later in the year. Beaver dams further enhance the storage capacity of the flood plain. Higher flows give dimension and pattern to the stream and redefine the channel. Vegetative debris and sediments that accumulated the previous year are redistributed downstream and to the edges of the stream to build up the banks so that grasses and woody vegetation gain a stronghold to further buffer succeeding floods.

The increase in discharge and warming water temperature during the spring rejuvenate surface algae, diatoms, mosses, vascular plants, and biofilms. During this time, the emergence of many aquatic insects such as mayflies, stoneflies, caddisflies, midges, and crane flies is triggered. These organisms complete their life cycles as reproducing aerial adults that disperse along the watercourse to eventually deposit eggs in the water to begin a new generation. Some of these insects will become food for fish and for riparian birds, mammals, amphibians, and other insects attracted to the aquatic habitat and the riparian vegetation. An increase in spring stream flow is also a signal for spawning by salmonids such as the Rio Grande cutthroat trout, which utilize cleaned stream bottom gravels.

Discharge begins to taper off after a few weeks of spring runoff. Summer flows generally are more stable, but can be interrupted by occasional floods. Monsoon rains later in the summer may cause temporary increases in volume. Flow and temperature decrease in late fall as precipitation decreases. Leaves falling into the water accumulate to form the food base for many aquatic organisms sustaining them through the winter. Snow accrued in the winter eventually melts in the spring to begin the runoff cycle again.

In an urban setting such as Santa Fe, summer rain and subsequent flooding is usually short lived, dramatic, and often times devastating. The impervious and built upon watershed acts as a shield, allowing the water to rush downstream through the previously dry and poorly vegetated arroyos and river channel. It is only when rushing water reaches the Santa Fe River Rural Protection Zone (originally the Santa Fe River Preserve) several miles downstream (below the City of Santa Fe Waste Water Treatment Plant discharge) that the riparian vegetation and expansive flood plain function as a cushion, buffering the flow. Here, high flows are absorbed and diverted throughout the bosque to later appear, diminished but sustained, to augment flow to the river downstream. Today, this phenomenon does not occur along the dry Santa Fe River near the downstream city limits of Santa Fe.

Seep that re-wets a section of the Santa Fe River near Patrick Smith Park. Photograph by A. Kyce Bello.

Through rivers, a variety of ecological communities are connected by the flow from headwater to lower elevations. In Santa Fe County, diverse neighborhoods, each with specific and perhaps different relationships to the river, are also intertwined. For most of the year the Santa Fe River through town and downstream is a dry remnant of its former self, visited and enjoyed by only a few. One only has to look to the community events celebrating the river when it occasionally flows in spring and summer to see how running water is cherished and appreciated. The river blessing at San Ysidro Crossing in Aqua Fria and the fishing derby and river festival within Santa Fe are well attended. A year round living Santa Fe River could provide an environment for play and exploration of the outdoors, linking neighborhoods through parks and the river trail and providing sustenance to nature. Once a living Santa Fe River is re-established, I would like to be involved in ecological studies. I want to take friends old and new to the river to turn over a few stones to see signs of the return, and encourage continuation of the numerous school projects showing our young people various positive aspects of the river. I hope such experiences will spur others to be as fascinated as I have always been with the life found in a river.

A Santa Fe resident for over 30 years, Gerald Z. Jacobi is Professor Emeritus of Environmental Science and Management at New Mexico Highlands University. He has also worked for state and federal resource agencies and is currently engaged in research projects with the New Mexico Department of Game and Fish, New Mexico Environment Department, U. S. Forest Service, and Trout Unlimited. He is a member of the Santa Fe River Commission.

River Song

Marcia Muth

A river runs past my house
Sometimes noisy, filled bank to bank
Sometimes quiet, low and slow-moving
Always there and always changing;
It is my calendar of the seasons,
This river that runs through my life.

Now that it is summer, hot, sunny
The wide river swims with fish
Varicolored scales flashing, looping
In magical, enchanted patterns;
Above the water flying insects
Cling together in hanging clouds
That move along like balloons,
The deep sound of the Bach Suites
Comes from my neighbor's house
While two butterflies dance aloft.

In the autumn leaves fall and float
On the river's surface, going fast
Toward some certain destination
Like a thousand small offerings
Of thanks or beseeching prayers;
The last bird songs are heard
Frogs mourn the passing days,
Cicadas singing predicts winter
My neighbor now plays Elgar
And the wind whispers of melancholy.

Snow covers ground, trees, stones
Standing by the river, I listen
For the familiar sound of water
But the river is ice-bound now
Yet I know that under the ice

The river still flows sluggishly;
My breath-cloud mimics the sky
Overcast, a colorless cloudiness
Then I hear the music of winter,
Creaking of wood in the cold air
Sighing of ice as it forms and re-forms,
The crunching under fast-moving feet
Eager to return to house-warmth.

In the spring winter comes rushing
Down the river's usual course,
Fed by melting mountain snows
And early warm welcoming rains
Little clumps of green appear
All along the water's edge;
There is the joy and sweetness
Of many remembered tiny flowers
Now with windows and doors open
I hear Beethoven spilling out
From my neighbor's house and yard.

~~~

Artist and poet Marcia Muth was born in Fort Wayne, Indiana in 1919 and moved to Santa Fe, New Mexico in 1966. "River Song" was originally published in *Words and Images*, her fourth book of poetry.

Cottonwoods and willows planted along the river replace older trees whose roots no longer reach the diminished water table. Photograph by EC Ryan.

Wisdom of the River

Ann Filemyr

"Rivers are the arteries of our Mother the Earth," explained elder Keewaydinoquay, an Anishinaabe mashkikiwe (Ojibwe herbal medicine woman). "The rivers are her blood. It is how she keeps her body clean and balanced transporting food and energy from one place to another, just like our arteries do."

She pointed with her lips at the dirty water choked with trash as we stood together on the bank of the Milwaukee River. I scrambled down the muddy embankment to untangle a plastic six-pack ring from the debris.

"When we dam the river, we block the healing flow. Do you think it is an accident that in our own bodies, our arteries and veins are blocked and dying? We are a mirror of our mother, the earth. Her body is our body. What we have done to her we have done to ourselves."

I spent that day and many others reaching in and cleaning up, slogging through muck to pick out cans, bottle, boxes, bags, rusted mattress springs, the discarded waste of our daily lives. In doing so, I hummed a prayer. The heart of this prayer is quite simple. *All the water that ever was and all the water that ever will be, is now, is here now. Bless the water.*

Water is part of a closed earth system, which we exist within. Water cycles around us and through us—tears, sweat, urine, blood—we mammals are mostly water. Water exists beneath us in underground wells and aquifers; above us in clouds, mist, fog, rain, snow, hail; and around us in seas, oceans, rivers, streams, pools, hot springs. It is the same water that has been on earth since the beginning. It is the same water rising up and falling back down. No water can be added. None can be taken away.

In the Ifé tradition of West Africa still practiced in parts of Brazil, the river is sacred to the Goddess Oxum, birth mother, lover, sacred dancer, life-bringer. Flowers honor her. Once I participated in a ceremony for Oxum in which we filled small cocoanut half shells with honey and yellow blossoms. Then we lifted our skirts and walked into the river and set these small shell boats adrift as a praise song for the river's life-giving power.

Throughout Europe, the old great cathedrals were built above springs once considered to be sacred to the Moon Goddess Diana. I remember in the south of France walking down stone stairs into a clammy vault beneath the floor of one such ancient church. There, hidden from view, in a cleft of moss-covered rock, a tiny spring trickled out and down into a stone pool. This water is then gathered up and used as holy water by the Catholic priests.

Across the arid Southwest, the first peoples still honor the sacred places where springs well up from beneath the earth. They return as their ancestors have done for thousands and thousands of years to sing the songs and perform the rites. Tomorrow morning one of our students at the Institute of American Indian Arts will join his Pueblo community dancing on the soft earth of their plaza as they celebrate the Cloud Dance at Ohkay Owingey.

There is a simple explanation for this veneration. Human beings are utterly and completely dependent upon water. Without water, there is no life. We are part of water's journey from earth to sky and back. Water is part of our journey from birth to death and back. Without the river, there is no human community. Only arrogance or ignorance allows us to dismiss this fact.

Rivers were once the roadways of the world. Before the wheel was the paddle and whatever kind of tree one had could be made into a boat. Water travel was the primary means of getting from place to place. And within the water lived abundant food. Ask any fisherman what the best food is. And along the river's banks grow the basketmaker's materials. In all of these and so many other ways water is source — not resource. Source of food. Source of movement. Source of life.

Wherever we stand on this earth, we stand in relation to the sea. The rivers mark the way. As a child growing up outside Philadelphia near the Delaware River, I could trace the simple path to the Chesapeake Bay and out into the Atlantic. When my family moved to Sheboygan County, Wisconsin I found the water route from the ocean came down the St. Lawrence Seaway, that waterline between the U.S. and Canada. It flows into Lake Ontario, then on over the enormous thundering falls at Niagara into Lake Erie, then up through Lake Huron and in a magnificent arc of blue-green shimmering at the Straits of Mackinac, the water flows into my lake, Lake Michigan.

When I left the North Country and moved to southern Ohio, I traced the waterpath from the spring that gave the town its name, Yellow Springs. I stood at the place where ice-cold water charges straight out of a limestone wall falling into a green creek. I followed the creek to the Little Miami River. Then traced the path of the Little Miami, named for the Miami Indians who call this land their home. It drops into the Ohio River, that old freedom line dividing the slave states of the south from the free states of the north. The Ohio spills into the Mississippi flowing steadily south toward the Gulf of Mexico.

When I moved to Santa Fe in 2005, I looked for my waterpath to the sea and found it creeping beneath enormous cottonwoods, the trickling waterway called the Santa Fe River. It begins in the rocky slopes above the city. Fed by winter snow, lush until the flat heat of summer dries it to a shadow. It whispers downhill past old adobe homes and west across the mesa to the bosque where it disappears into the Rio Grande, that ancient roadway of trade, that sandhill crane thoroughfare, the major path of migratory birds. Then the Rio Grande veers back toward the rising sun, marking the wounded divide between the U.S. and Mexico, until it fans out into the saltwater of the Gulf.

Once I know where I am in relation to the sea, I have my bearings. I can live anywhere and be at home. Though this may be a personal idiosyncrasy, bioregionalists regard a basic knowledge of one's watershed as fundamental to an environmental ethic. Barry Lopez in his essay, *The Naturalist*, reflects on his relationship to the McKenzie River in western Oregon. He states: "Almost every day I go down to the river with no intention but to sit and watch. I have been watching the river for thirty years, just the three or four hundred yards of it I can see from the forested bank, a run of clear, quick water about 350 feet wide. If I have learned anything here, it's that each time I come down, something I don't know yet will reveal itself."

Here is a unique reason to renew our waterway. The promise that each time we go to the river, sit and observe, something new may reveal itself. Learning directly from nature is an ancient kind of wisdom, one shared by field biologists, poets, philosophers, and indigenous elders who believe it is in these wild places that we may seek insight into the riddle of our existence.

Close up of the Santa Fe River. Photograph by EC Ryan.

The Santa Fe River is rarely acknowledged as a potential source of wisdom. We may walk alongside it, strolling beneath the old cottonwoods, the traffic of Alameda on one side, the dry ditch that was once a river disappearing down a steep bank on the other. But at what point along this urban path are we invited to stop, sit, reflect, watch the river, the sky, breathe, learn, and be? Only along Canyon Road are there a few discreet benches that face the river. Most of the benches actually face the street instead of the river. We even forget to think that the canyon for which Canyon Road is named was formed by the river. I sat on one of the street-facing benches recently and it struck me. We have literally turned our backs on the river.

Santa Fe is a community that appreciates diverse thinkers. We are home to a multiplicity of cultural and spiritual traditions. Most of these incorporate reverence for the natural world. St. Francis of Assisi, the patron saint of Santa Fe, saw wildlife as an expression of the Divine. Yet our collective awareness of the river as a vital presence running through the heart of town is lacking.

Every great city is on the shore of a great river. From Minneapolis to St. Louis to New Orleans, the big muddy Mississippi rolls. Manhattan floats between the Hudson and the East Rivers. Paris has the Seine, London the Thames, and Alexandria rises up in the Nile delta. Shanghai would not be without the Yangtze. Baghdad is tied to the Tigris. And the city of Santa Fe is here because of a river.

Without a healthy river, how long can a city survive? How is it that our city's river has become so neglected as to be nearly extinct? Even the post-industrial cities of the Great Lakes whose rivers were once declared dead have become conscientious caretakers of their rivers. Let us look to Cleveland, Detroit, and Milwaukee for examples of waterway revitalization.

The infamous burning of the Cuyahoga River in 1969 is not forgotten by Cleveland citizens. Today they hold an annual Great Lakes Burning River Fest featuring environmental organizations, green companies, sustainable farmers and restaurants. The event is held at The Nautica Entertainment Complex with scenic views of the riverfront and serves as a living exhibit of the river's environmental and economic impact on the community. The Cuyahoga is cleaner, safer, and more beautiful than it was only a few decades ago.

Detroit has established one of the first "blueways." Like a greenbelt, it is an intentional space created in an urban site for human-nature interplay. The blueway water trail invites canoeists, kayakers, sailboaters, and others to travel the Detroit Heritage River Water Trail, the first such blueway established along a river designated by both the U.S. and Canada as a Heritage River.

The Milwaukee Riverkeeper's mission is to protect water quality and wildlife habitat in the river corridors and to advocate for sound land use in the Milwaukee, Menomonee and Kinnickinnic River watersheds. Volunteers join "Watershed Action Teams" to monitor clean-up efforts and educate the public on the vital importance of clean rivers in this densely populated area. The Milwaukee

Riverkeeper is a licensed member of the Waterkeeper Alliance, a national coalition dedicated to protecting and restoring our nation's waterways.

These cities have established opportunities for citizens to turn around and face their rivers. They have made these rivers once again a source of inspiration and celebration. If they can do it, certainly we can.

The Pueblos of New Mexico began beside the riverbanks and continue to flourish beside their flow. Early Hispanic settlers managed the acequia system with precise attention to preserve and protect the river systems. It is time for Santa Fe to reclaim this commitment. Like any neglected relationship, our river will not survive without loving attention and action.

Santa Fe is a creative community and as other cities have done, we too, can restore our river. Leading this effort is the Santa Fe Watershed Association. They are dedicated to reviving the river "from the dry ditch it is today to a flowing, vibrant perennial stream...Our dream is a flowing, meandering, tree-lined stream where fish and frogs can swim, children can play...Our mission is to return the Santa Fe River to a living river from the headwaters in the Sangre de Cristo to the Rio Grande." Educators, artists, community leaders, youth and scientists should come together in this common purpose. What may be learned from our river should entice us.

Lopez learned from his river that, "local flora and fauna are pieces of an inscrutable mystery, increasingly deep, a unity of organisms."

We are a living part of this mysterious unity.

Ann Filemyr, PhD, moved to Santa Fe to serve as Dean of the Center for Arts & Cultural Studies at the Institute of American Indian Arts from Antioch College in Ohio in 2005. She is dedicated to opening pathways for indigenous knowledge to infuse mainstream culture. She is a writer, sweetgrass gardener, artist, and educator.

Water and Faith

from *People of the Valley*
Frank Waters

Frank Water's 1941 novel People of the Valley *tells the epic story of Maria del Valle, herb woman and matriarch of a small New Mexican village facing the threats of modernity. As her people are forced off their land to make way for a dam, Maria reflects upon the deep currents of faith and the "unseen flows" that cannot be obstructed.*

~~~

It was el Día de San Juan de Bautista, and she had kept the faith.

On this day all the waters of the earth are blessed, the seas, the rivers and the ritos, the clear forest streams and all the muddy acequias meandering through the fields. So at break of day you must go down to the stream and bathe. Thus you will be immersed in the one living mystery, the waters of life blessed by St. John the Baptist, he who baptized the Cristo Himself.

For this day all week you have hoed your weeds, prepared your fields that San Juan, the patron of waters, may favor your crops. Now this is the sign of his blessing to them and to you, who need equally the waters of life to grow and prosper, that at four o'clock, according to custom, it rains.

Water is like life. It is life. It permeates everything. The hand of God drops it at birth. It trickles down the snowy peaks, the little streams feed rito and acequia, the great rivers rush down to the sea. And the deep sea too feeds with mist and vapor that great blue lake of life unseen by us all, to be renewed again and ever.

What is life without water? What is life without faith? So all the waters of the earth are blessed, and all the flesh of the earth is permeated by its flow, and all the earth of the flesh is sanctified by faith.

For faith is not a concept. It is not a form. It is a baptism in the one living mystery of ever-flowing life, and it must be renewed as life itself is ever renewed.

This is the meaning of any dam, that it would obstruct the free flow of faith which renews and refreshes life and gives it its only meaning. It is self-enclosing. It means stagnation. It means death.

Faith is not to be dammed. It is not to be measured and meted out when timely. It must be free to penetrate every cell and germ of the whole. For it is the obstructed whole that finally bursts the dam, brings destruction and misery, swamps the temporal benefits of the past.

There are dams. There will be more. But all are temporal and unwhole. For they, like us, are spattered, swept and undercut by an unseen flow — a flow that is longer than casual benefits, that never ceases to permeate and undermine our lesser faiths, and which can never be truly dammed.

Prayer in Time of Drought

Lonnie Howard

The river has been rushing for days now
reservoir overflowing, gates opened
running for days now cold clear tumbling
over rock; Santa Fe River rushing
into the Rio Grande into the Gulf of Mexico
into the great body of ocean
evaporating becoming cloud rolling
over this green blue jewel spinning
through space becoming rain becoming

snow heavy on mountaintop
cold silent

until sunlight is long enough and high enough
to turn snow to trickling water drop by drop
it surges into winding creeks filling
the reservoir again and the gates open
and the river flows again cold clear tumbling
over rock flowing into ocean becoming
clouds rolling over this blue green jewel spinning
through space. Dark clouds roll across the sky

break open and pour their grace on this mountain
again and again
and again

cc

Lonnie Howard lives near the Acequia Madre, two blocks from the Santa Fe River. She is the director of the Scherer Institute of Natural Healing and is an avid birder. Her poems have appeared in the *Santa Fe Literary Review*, and other journals, as well as in the anthology *Earthships: A New Mecca Poetry Collection*.

Run, river, run. Photograph by EC Ryan.

Appendix A

Chronology of Key Santa Fe River Events
Don Goldman

1609   Pedro de Peralta moves capital of New Mexico to Santa Fe

1846   U.S. forces occupy Santa Fe. Two army engineers explore the Rito de Santa Fe to its source and recommend construction of a dam

1880   Santa Fe Water & Improvement Co. granted "The exclusive right and privilege of erecting dams and impounding water on the Santa Fe River" by Santa Fe County Commissioners

1881   Old Stone Dam built with a capacity of 25 acre-feet

1890   Santa Fe's population reaches 6,185
       Water flows to city residents through mains

1893   Two-Mile Dam built with a capacity approximately 387 acre-feet

1895   Hydroelectric plant and Talaya reservoir built

1900   Santa Fe's population drops to 5,603

1902   High Line ditch constructed

1904   Flood fills Old Stone Reservoir
       By-pass tunnel around Two-Mile Reservoir replaced by open channel

1910   Santa Fe's population is 5,072

1914   Citizens of Santa Fe petition the State Engineer to confirm their water rights to the Santa Fe River
       There are 38 ditches in Santa Fe, irrigating approximately 1300 acres

1920   Santa Fe's population grows to 7,236

1925   Record low flow in Santa Fe River to 1,780 acre-feet

1926   Granite Point Dam (McClure) built with a capacity of approximately 650 acre-feet
       Power plant removed sometime prior to 1926

1930 Santa Fe's population reaches 11,176
      Public Works Administration builds concrete bridges across river, deepens river
      bed and lines it with rock
      After meters were installed, water use declined in spite of population increase
      Period of rapid population growth
      Debris fence ("tin ditch") constructed

1932 Lower watershed closed to public to protect water supply

1935 McClure capacity increased to 3,059 acre-feet

1940 Santa Fe's population is 20,325

1942 Army hospital built, increased water demand

1943 Nichols Dam built with a capacity of approximately 684 acre-feet
      High Line ditch abandoned

1946 First two wells drilled in Santa Fe
      PNM created

1947 City plagued by low storage capacity in spite of new Nichols Reservoir
      McClure capacity increased

1950 Santa Fe's population reaches 28,000
      New record low flow in Santa Fe River of 1,530 acre-feet
      Third well drilled

1951 Three more wells drilled in Santa Fe
      City begins planning for San Juan-Chama water

1960 Santa Fe's population increases to 33,400

1961 Santa Fe filed for 5,605 acre-feet per year of San Juan-Chama water rights
      Seventh well drilled

1963 Water quality issues in reservoir

1970 Population is 41,167
      Eighth well drilled

1971 Association of Santa Fe Acequias formed

1972 Buckman wells drilled 15 miles northwest of Santa Fe

1975 Water treatment plant built
      Two-Mile becomes back-up supply

1977 There are seven functioning acequias in Santa Fe

1978 Two-Mile listed as hazardous

1980 Santa Fe's population grows to 49,299

1989 PNM claims ownership of all water rights in the river, opposes having to release water to the acequias

1990 Population is 55,859
Judge Art Encinias states acequia rights antedate PNM and orders water released

1992 Two-Mile drained for safety

1994 Two-Mile breached after 101 years

1995 PNM sells Sangre de Cristo Water Company to Santa Fe
McClure capacity increased to 3,325 acre-feet

2000 Population is 62,200
PNM donates 188 acres to The Nature Conservancy

2002 Santa Fe Canyon Preserve opens

2003 There are four functioning acequias in Santa Fe
Water use in Santa Fe is about 12,000 acre-feet per year

2007 American Rivers names Santa Fe River most endangered river in the United States due to severe lack of water

Appendix B

What is a Living River?
Santa Fe River Commission

What does a living river look like? Advocates of the Santa Fe River use this question to guide their decisions about river restoration. Here are some of the elements that the Santa Fe River Commission has determined constitute a living river.

A living river is one that supports life and is the clearest expression of a healthy watershed. Life depends on water, and water in a high desert environment is perhaps the most valuable resource

A living river in a high desert environment is a corridor that carries perennial or ephemeral flows (dependent on variable weather patterns)

Between intermittent flows, refuge pools in a living river are critical to the survival of biological organisms (like fish, birds, and insects)

A living river in this highly variable environment is also subject to flood regimes that create the conditions under which many plant and animal species reproduce, including New Mexico's most important riparian tree, the cottonwood

In an urban setting, a living river's flood regime must be balanced with a municipality's need to protect the community from floods

If connected to its watershed (including an urban community's storm water system that encourages infiltration), a living river may be a perennially wetted corridor on which plants' roots depend, in which animals take refuge, and from which humans draw sustenance and enjoyment

A living river has a bed and banks of soil in which plants roots can grow and is accessible to passersby, since the distance between the river bank and river bed is not too great

A living river experiences regular, if intermittent, flows, has a wetted bed, and supports a healthy plant community that resists down-cutting and severe erosion

A living river occasionally needs room to meander as the nature of rivers is stability in lateral mobility, which is possible in limited reaches of the Santa Fe River

A living river connects varied ecological communities as it connects diverse human neighborhoods

A living river provides a rich environment for children's play, for youthful exploration of the outdoors and serves as open space that links neighborhoods and parks and places of work

A living river is a refuge for all in the community—free of trash and illegal activity

A living river is a treasured resource cherished by its community

Appendix C

HOUSE JOINT MEMORIAL 3
49TH LEGISLATURE - STATE OF NEW MEXICO - FIRST SESSION, 2009
INTRODUCED BY
Mimi Stewart

No area of water is more important to the future of our state than the business of protecting the water that flows in our streams. Unfortunately, many rivers are already impaired and our state has no real program for protecting rivers from over-development. HJM 3 created a process of considering how we might protect our rivers. While the Senate did not pass it during the 2009 legislature due to time restrictions, Rep. Stewart continues to work to move it forward by collaborating with state agencies to incorporate these principles into their policies.

A JOINT MEMORIAL
REQUESTING THE WATER CABINET DEPARTMENTS TO CONDUCT AN ENVIRONMENTAL FLOW ASSESSMENT TO ENHANCE ECOSYSTEM FUNCTION, FISH AND WILDLIFE HABITAT AND IMPROVED MANAGEMENT OF RESERVOIRS, WITH THE COLLABORATION OF RELEVANT SCIENTISTS AND STAKEHOLDERS, FEDERAL AGENCIES AND WATER USERS.

WHEREAS, New Mexico's rivers are a keystone of the state's environmental infrastructure; and

WHEREAS, the flow of water in New Mexico's rivers is directly tied to economic prosperity, water supply, agricultural production, cultural diversity, community viability and the health of people and ecosystems; and

WHEREAS, seasonal high-flow events reduce frequency of bosque fires by sweeping combustible debris from river floodplains and continually wetted channels provide flood mitigation by storing and attenuating high flows; and

WHEREAS, natural infiltration from river flows recharges aquifers, thereby enhancing water security during drought cycles; and

WHEREAS, the advance of invasive aquatic and riparian species and the decline of native species, due in part to altered hydrology, have come to characterize New Mexico's river basins; and

WHEREAS, further indicators of declining ecosystem health are manifest in each of the state's river systems, in the form of federally listed threatened and endangered species, whose conservation and recovery require costly, long-term programs; and

WHEREAS, state management actions to maintain or enhance the hydrography of the state's river systems to prevent future environmental losses or listings of native species will keep control of these issues in state agencies; and

WHEREAS, New Mexico lacks any system for environmental flow considerations in its water management practices; and

WHEREAS, predicted changes in climate coupled with continuing increases in human needs for water can only magnify the stress on the healthy functioning of river systems and may potentially result in future water supply shortages, interregional and interstate conflicts and serious economic and ecological distress;

NOW, THEREFORE, BE IT RESOLVED BY THE LEGISLATURE OF THE STATE OF NEW MEXICO that the policy of the state of New Mexico be to bring the maintenance of adequate environmental flows into the water management practices on its river systems; and

BE IT FURTHER RESOLVED that in furtherance of this policy, the legislature request all the state departments represented in the water cabinet to work cooperatively in preparation of an environmental flow assessment to evaluate and prioritize areas in need of improved flow management, identifying stream segments where flow management might result in significant ecological benefits, including preservation of fish and wildlife habitat and environmental quality and areas where benefits can be realized through improved reservoir management; and

BE IT FURTHER RESOLVED that the evaluation shall identify suitable alternative methods for determining environmental flow needs in New Mexico and be conducted in collaboration with relevant specialists, federal agencies and water users; and

BE IT FURTHER RESOLVED that copies of this memorial be transmitted to all cabinet secretaries whose departments are represented on the water cabinet and to the interstate stream commission.

Continued Reading and Resources

Clark, Ira G. *Water in New Mexico: A History of its Management and Use.* Albuquerque: University of New Mexico Press, 1987.

Crawford, Stanley. *The River in Winter: New and Selected Essays.* Albuquerque: University of New Mexico Press, 2003.

Currant, Nanda. *Riverworks: Performance and Community Art for Rivers.* Published by the author, 2008.

Goldman, Don. *The Santa Fe River and Its Water.* Santa Fe: The Nature Conservancy in New Mexico, 2003.

Grant, Paige. "Santa Fe Watershed Restoration Action Strategy," 2002. http://www. nmenv.state.nm.us/swqb/Santa_Fe_WRAS-2002.pdf

Lancaster, Brad. *Rainwater Harvesting for Drylands, Volume 1: Guiding Principles to Welcome Rain Into Your Life and Landscape.* Tucson, AZ: Rainsource Press, 2006.

Plewa, Tara. "Acequia Agriculture: Water, Irrigation, and Their Defining Roles in Santa Fe History." *Santa Fe: History of an Ancient City.* Edited by David Grant Noble. Santa Fe: School for Advanced Research Press, 2008.

Postel, Sandra and Brian Richter. *Rivers for Life: Managing Water for People and Nature.* Washington, DC: Island Press, 2003.

Rivera, José A. *Acequia Culture: Water, Land, and Community in the Southwest.* Albuquerque: University of New Mexico Press, 1998.

Snow, David H. *The Santa Fe Acequia Systems: Summary Report of their History and Present Status, with Recommendations for Use and Protection.* Santa Fe: City of Santa Fe, 1988.

American Rivers
www.americanrivers.org
American Rivers is a leading national organization standing up for healthy rivers so communities can thrive. Through national advocacy, innovative solutions and a growing network of strategic partners, they protect and promote rivers as valuable assets that are vital to our health, safety and quality of life. Their website includes resources to aid communities in protecting and promoting their rivers.

City of Santa Fe
www.santafenm.gov
The Governing body of the City of Santa Fe has taken the following steps to restore the Santa Fe River and Watershed: Revived the River Commission; directed staff to

include water for the river into the long-range water supply plan; hired a full time River and Watershed Coordinator; undertaken an environmental flow study to determine flows necessary to support a living river; contracted with Santa Fe's Youth for job skills training to work on erosion, vegetation, and restoration improvements in the watershed; worked jointly with the County and designers to prepare restoration plans for up to 8 miles of the river corridor; contracted with the SF Watershed Association for the Adopt-a-River program since 2002; begun construction on a multi-use trail adjacent to the Santa Fe River; diversified the purpose of flood releases to support the river ecosystem; and created the Santa Fe River Fund to buy or lease water rights for the river. Santa Fe's long-range water plan, confirmed in September 2008, addresses the future of water use in Santa Fe and identifies a sustainable and reliable water supply. It can be found at www.santafenm.gov/index.asp?NID=1030

Instream Flow Council

www.instreamflowcouncil.org

The Instream Flow Council (IFC) is an organization that represents the interests of state and provincial fish and wildlife management agencies in the United States and Canada dedicated to improving the effectiveness of their instream flow programs. The Instream Flow Council has developed a number of resources valuable in understanding the legal, scientific, and practical issues associated with providing adequate water for fish, wildlife and other ecological needs, and made them available through their website.

New Mexican Riparian Council

www.ripariancouncil.org

The New Mexican Riparian Council is an organization dedicated to "the continued survival, maintenance, and enhancement of riparian systems in New Mexico for further benefit and enjoyment of present and future generation." The council educates the public on riparian issues and supports communities in developing restoration and conservation tools for their wetlands.

River Source

www.riversource.net

River Source supports people living as good stewards of their watersheds through education in watershed science, providing restoration services, and promoting collaboration. Their website offers numerous links to resources on watershed monitoring, including a watershed health database and interactive USGS map that shows real time river flow data for rivers across the state.

Santa Fe Watershed Association

www.santafewatershed.org

The Santa Fe Watershed Association is working to restore the Santa Fe River and its watershed through advocacy, education, hands-on restoration work, and a growing network of partners. They advocate for policies that will restore the Santa Fe River to a level of ecological health that sustains aquatic life, wildlife, trees and plants, and our ground water. Their programs both restore and build support for a living river through education and activities that connect people to the river. Their website includes reports on environmental flow policies in New Mexico, and other relevant topics.

Permissions

CPSIA information can be obtained at www.ICGtesting.com

226311LV00001B/1/P